A

TO:

FROM:

Whatever you ask for in prayer, believe that you have received it, and it will be yours.

MARK 11:24

Daily Prayer from the New International Version

ISBN 0-310-98256-1

Requests for information should be addressed to:
Inspirio, The gift group of Zondervan
Grand Rapids, Michigan 49530
http://www.inspiriogifts.com

Associate Editor: Molly Detweiler
Written & Adapted by: Sarah M. Hupp
Design Manager: Amy E. Langeler
Designer: David Carlson

Printed in the United States of America

01 02 03/HK/ 3 2 1

DAILY PRAYER FROM THE NEW INTERNATIONAL VERSION

INTRODUCTION

A popular bumper sticker proclaims, "Prayer changes things." But does it really? Though the Bible reminds us to "pray continually" (1 Thessalonians 5:17), faithfully (Romans 12:12), and "on all occasions" (Ephesians 6:18), what exactly should we be praying for?

The Bible tells a story about David that helps answer these questions. The Amalekites had abducted David's family. Rather than react to a difficult situation in a haphazard way, 1 Samuel 30:6 says, "David found strength in the LORD his God." The account in 1 Samuel continues by telling us that David prayed specifically about his need, asking God whether or not he should pursue the Amalekites and whether or not he would be successful in his venture. Because David took the time to seek God, he didn't act in haste. And because David had prayed so specifically, God's direct answers gave the guidance David needed to rescue his family.

David realized an important lesson about prayer in this situation: If we fail to pray with a specific focus, we can miss God's outstretched hand of willingness to deliver us from our troubles and concerns. Throughout the rest of his life, David continued to make his specific requests known to God and awaited God's answer with a believing spirit.

Following David's example in prayer, the pages of this prayer guide use a weekly repeating format to help you center your prayers on your spiritual life, your friends and family, church and community, specific areas of the world, and the wonders of God. As you pray each day, seeking direct answers and listening for God's heart in prayer, you'll find the fire of great faith and carry away a basketful of blessings, both for yourself and others. Such prayer *will* change things! May you truly "devote yourselves to prayer, being watchful and thankful" (Colossians 4:2).

S.M.H.

FORGIVEN BY GOD

"I will forgive their wickedness and will remember their sins no more," says the Lord.

HEBREWS 8:12

One of the greatest blessings God has given us is the promise of forgiveness. Though we fail time and again, God is faithful to forgive us when we confess our sins. This confession is not merely a recitation of our obvious mistakes, but also a recognition of our willful choices and our disobedience to God's ways. When we bring these failings to the light of God's love, the Bible tells us that God not only forgives those sins, he also forgets them. What a blessing it is to be forgiven by God!

S.M.H.

AS YOU PRAY TODAY:

- Bring your failures and mistakes to God.
- Receive the gift of God's forgiveness.
- Rejoice in God's loving forgetfulness.

RELATIVE GRATEFULNESS

As we have opportunity, let us do good to all people, especially to those who belong to the family of believers.

GALATIANS 6:10

A child's bedtime prayers often consist of a "God bless" list that names every relative, pet, or acquaintance the child can remember. As we grow up, our prayer list expands. But we should never stop being grateful for our families. We receive many things from them—the color of our eyes, the cowlicks in our hair, and our viewpoints and attitudes about life. Our families would not be complete without any one of us!

S.M.H.

AS YOU PRAY TODAY:

- Thank God for your immediate family (mom, dad, brothers, sisters). Name them one by one.
- Praise God for your extended family (grandparents, aunts, uncles, cousins).
- Find specific reasons to be thankful for each family member.

HANGING ON THE WALL

"I will give you shepherds after my own heart, who will lead you," says the LORD.

JEREMIAH 3:15

A little girl watched an ordination service in a small church. Puzzled, she whispered, "Daddy, we're supposed to install the new pastor today. But where are the screws to hang him on the wall?"

Though her question may seem comical, pastors sometimes find themselves hung by their parishioners on walls of judgmentalism. If a pastor doesn't preach stirring sermons every week, someone will complain. If the sick aren't visited or a meeting runs late, the pastor may receive a reprimand. Yet pastors are God's leaders. When we install our pastors, God wants us to love them.

S.M.H.

AS YOU PRAY TODAY:

- Pray for your pastor's time—time for prayer, study, and worship.
- Ask God for wisdom to prioritize family and ministry concerns.
- Pray for your pastor's health, safety, and protection from temptation.

A TALL ORDER

"Seek the peace and prosperity of the city to which I have carried you," says the LORD.

JEREMIAH 29:7

In 1900 there were only 11 cities in the world with a population of over a million. Now there are over 150 such cities. It is the responsibility of the mayor in each of these cities to oversee their administration and to care for the welfare of each inhabitant. That's a tall order. Whether you reside in a small township or a large city, your mayor or township official carries a heavy burden of responsibility that grows with each additional citizen and each passing year.

S.M.H.

AS YOU PRAY TODAY:

- Intercede for your mayor's moral character—integrity and a clear knowledge of right and wrong.
- Beseech God's wisdom and guidance in the decisions your mayor must make.
- Pray God's protection for your city leader.

GOOD NEWS FOR THE JUNGLE

How beautiful are the feet of those who bring good news!

ROMANS 10:15

Venezuela is a modern country in South America, well known for the highest waterfall in the world (Angel Falls) and for some of the largest oilfields in the world, too. Yet within Venezuela's southeastern rain forests live the Yanomamo Indians. They are a fierce, warlike tribe who are fearful of strangers and know little about the world beyond their thatched homes and jungle life. Enslaved by generations of superstition and witchcraft, the Yanomamo Indians need to hear God's Good News of salvation.

AS YOU PRAY TODAY:

- Ask God to give Christian workers insight into the Yanomamo culture to help open their hearts to Christ.
- Pray that the Yanomamo will learn to read the Bible portions that have been translated into their language.
- Because of their jungle isolation, intercede for protection for the missionaries and the Yanomamo.

JUST BECAUSE!

Praise the L*ORD* *for his surpassing greatness.*

PSALM 150:2

A little boy ran into the kitchen, grabbed his mother's knees and proclaimed, "You're the best-est Mom in the whole world!"

It wasn't her birthday, so the boy's remark took his mother by surprise. "Why do you say that?" she asked with a smile.

"No reason," he called as he ran outside. "Just because!"

We all appreciate being appreciated, especially when it's unexpected. But when was the last time we appreciated God? Not because he blessed us or took care of some problem. When was the last time we appreciated God—"just because"?

S.M.H.

AS YOU PRAY TODAY:

- Picture yourself hugging God's knees like a child. Then, smile and thank God for who he is.
- Praise God for his greatness, his faithfulness, his love, and his compassion. Sing your praise, if you like. God loves to hear you sing!

GOD'S TEMPLE

Your body is a temple of the Holy Spirit,
who is in you.

1 CORINTHIANS 6:19

Centennial Park in Nashville, Tennessee boasts an exact replica of the Parthenon. Visitors stare open-mouthed at the towering columns, ornate carvings, and massive stone blocks that recreate this temple to the Greek goddess Athena. Yet the Bible tells us that our bodies are more marvelous than this human monument to a mythical being. Our bodies are the temple of God's Holy Spirit. Though the original Parthenon housed a statue of Athena, our bodies house the Spirit of the living God. Our bodies are a place of worship, glory, honor, and awe—for the Holy Spirit resides within.

S.M.H.

AS YOU PRAY TODAY:

- Gratefully acknowledge God's presence in your life.
- Mindfully set yourself apart from things that could harm God's temple—your body.
- Ask God to show you ways to worship, glorify, and honor him with your body.

JONATHAN AND DAVID

Jonathan made a covenant with David because he loved him.

1 SAMUEL 18:3

When the first white settlers came to North America, they found the land already inhabited by the Indians. Though these Indians did not have a written alphabet, their vocabulary was as advanced as any of the new settlers. In fact, their understanding of friendship mirrored the biblical relationship between Jonathan and David. Jonathan and David's friendship grew out of a time of shared joys and shared troubles. The Indians' word for "friend" reflects that relationship for it can be roughly translated "the one who carries my sorrows on his back."

S.M.H.

AS YOU PRAY TODAY:

- Thank God for your friends. Name them individually.
- Pray a special blessing for each one—a blessing specifically tailored for that friend.
- Ask God to show you a way to encourage a friend today.

A BETTER TEACHER

Come, my children, listen to me;
I will teach you the fear of the LORD.

PSALM 34:11

At a Sunday School Convention in Chicago, Howard Hendricks met a lady from Upper Michigan. Hendricks discovered that she was in her 80s, taught a junior high boys' Sunday School class with 50 students, and had saved pennies to pay for a round-trip bus ticket so that she could attend the convention for a day. When Hendricks asked her why she would go to such trouble, the woman replied, "I came to learn something that would make me a better teacher." Her commitment humbled Hendricks and instilled in him a desire to become a better teacher too.

AS YOU PRAY TODAY:

- Ask God to provide dedicated, loving Sunday School teachers for the children in your family.
- Intercede for the teachers for uninterrupted time to prepare their weekly lessons.
- Pray that the teachers will grow in their understanding of God and be able to share that understanding with their students.

NOTORIOUS OR NOTEWORTHY

Submit yourselves for the Lord's sake … to governors.

1 PETER 2:13–14

The highest elected official in any state in the United States is its governor. Responsible for managing all departments of a state, many governors have found this position an invaluable training ground for the presidency. More than 45 percent of U.S. presidents have successfully governed their states or territories. Yet history books record corrupt governors as well as honorable ones. In the past two decades, governors have fallen from office for bribery, conspiracy, obstruction of justice, and misappropriation of funds. Your prayers may determine whether your governor's record will be notorious or noteworthy.

S.M.H.

AS YOU PRAY TODAY:

- Intercede for God's guidance in your governor's policy decisions.
- Pray God's protection for your governor—in areas of health and influence.
- Ask God to provide trustworthy friends who will hold your governor to godly standards of accountability.

A PERFECT SACRIFICE

Christ died for sins once for all,
the righteous for the unrighteous.

1 PETER 3:18

Myanmar, formerly known as Burma, is well acquainted with sacrifice and struggle. Governed by a military dictatorship, this union of seven districts and seven ethnic minorities adheres to Buddhism. Families often give their children away to Buddhist monasteries. According to Buddhist belief, this "sacrifice" earns family members a better chance for eternal life. Christian missionaries had been active in Myanmar prior to their expulsion in 1966. A remnant of believers exists, but finds severe government resistance to sharing the message of Christ.

AS YOU PRAY TODAY:

- Ask God to strengthen the Burmese believers in their faith.
- Pray that the message of Christ's sacrifice "once for all" will touch the unsaved.
- Intervene for a relaxation of governmental restrictions so that Burmese believers can share their faith more openly.

THINK AND THANK

We will tell the next generation the praiseworthy deeds of the LORD.

PSALM 78:4

Psalm 78 contains a brief history of the nation of Israel from the time of Jacob to the reign of King David. Woven throughout this Psalm are many indictments against God's people and their forgetfulness. Despite God's repeated miracles on their behalf, "they did not remember his power" (v. 42), but rather rebelled against him, disobeyed him, and constantly "put God to the test" (v. 56). The Psalmist realized that by consciously remembering the "praiseworthy deeds of the LORD" (v. 4), succeeding generations would not fall prey to these mistakes of their forefathers.

S.M.H.

AS YOU PRAY TODAY:

- Remember the things that God has done for us—the provision of a Savior, the beautiful world we live in, the love of your friends and family and all the other blessings of your life.
- Thank God specifically for the unexpected blessings he sends your way.
- Praise God for the evidences of his steadfast love and continuing care.

GOD'S CHILDREN

"You will be my sons and daughters," says the Lord Almighty.

2 CORINTHIANS 6:18

Wayne and Sherry opened their heart to a child through the process of adoption. They prepared a place in their home for him and expectantly awaited his arrival. And when the judge declared that the adoption was official, cheers erupted and smiles flooded the courtroom. Anthony was their son!

In a spiritual way, Anthony's experience is our own. God has opened his heart to us because of his great love for us. He has prepared a place for us to live with him, and he expectantly awaits our arrival (John 14:2–3). And when we become his children, the hosts of heaven rejoice (Luke 15:7). So, give a cheer! Hallelujah! We are God's children!

S.M.H.

AS YOU PRAY TODAY:

- Thank God for adopting you.
- Picture yourself in God's house in heaven.
- Ask God to care for you as a parent cares for a child.

MAGNETIC POLARITY

Whatever is admirable—if anything is excellent or praiseworthy—think about such things.

PHILIPPIANS 4:8

Children are fascinated with magnetic polarity. When two like ends of magnets are put together, the magnets push each other apart. But when a positive pole of a magnet is put against another magnet's negative pole, the magnets stick tight.

This magnetic lesson applies to families, too. If we focus on the negative things about a family member, our families will be pushed apart by criticism. But if we look for a positive quality in a family member who irritates us, we'll be drawn together and learn more about each other, too.

S.M.H.

AS YOU PRAY TODAY:

- Confess to God your negativism toward any family member. Be specific.
- Ask God to show you a positive quality in this individual, no matter how small.
- Pray that God will keep you focused on this praiseworthy quality. Leave negativism to magnets!

NO CLASS

The teaching of the wise is a fountain of life.

PROVERBS 13:14

John and Joanne visited a new church. The people were friendly and the service was uplifting. But the church had no adult Sunday School class. So, John and Joanne sat in the foyer and quietly began to discuss a Bible passage. A young man strolled by and asked if he could join them. Volunteers finished cleaning the kitchen and pulled up chairs, too. Before the hour was over, that impromptu Sunday School class held nine persons.

It didn't take seminary schooling or a master's degree in public speaking to sit and share the Bible that day. It only took a willing heart—and lives were changed forever.

S.M.H.

AS YOU PRAY TODAY:

- Thank God for your Sunday School teacher.
- Ask for a willing heart to share God's Word with others.
- Pray for an opportunity to become a Sunday School teacher.

SENATORS AND SALESCLERKS

God is not unjust; he will not forget your work and the love you have shown him as you have helped his people and continue to help them.

HEBREWS 6:10

He looked like any other guy that Saturday in the home improvement store. Wiggly children in his shopping cart stretched curious hands toward racks of screws while he studied a display of caulking. Yet this fellow was no ordinary guy. He was my state senator, and he needed my help. As I sent him away with the proper product in hand, he said thanks and pushed the cartload of children toward the door. And I realized, whether senator or salesclerk, we all need some help to get the job done. That help should begin with prayer.

S.M.H.

AS YOU PRAY TODAY:

- Thank God for your senators, whether you voted for them or not.
- Pray for your senator as you would pray for yourself: for guidance, safety, health, etc.
- Ask God to help you encourage your senator. Encouragement is as needed as political feedback.

SUDAN'S JIHAD

Pray for us, too, that God may open a door for our message.

COLOSSIANS 4:3

The largest country in Africa is involved in an unholy war. Since 1985, the Muslim government in northern Sudan has declared war against the mostly Christian southern section of the country. Since its beginning, more than two million people have been slaughtered in this bitter jihad. Millions more are at risk. Families in the south are terrorized—fathers killed, mothers raped, and children taken into slavery. Entire villages have been wiped out by disease. Famine is widespread. Western nations are slowly awakening to this situation and sending aid. But the war and persecution continues.

AS YOU PRAY TODAY:

- Intercede for the salvation of Sudanese leaders.
- Pray God's protection for those who deliver aid packets.
- Ask God to keep the believers in Sudan strong in their faith. May they have opportunities to share the Gospel with their persecutors and see positive results.

A NEW SONG

Praise God for his acts of power.
PSALM 150:2

Have you ever thanked God for the wonderful things he has done for you? Eugene Peterson says that the book of Psalms concludes with a "cannonade of praise. Booming salvos of joy shake the air. Every creature is enlisted as a voice in the climactic chorus. There is not a shred of timidity in them, not a vestige of solemnity—they whirl in dance and raise exuberant songs of praise as they use every resource of voice and body to express delight in the God who delights in them."

AS YOU PRAY TODAY:

- Acknowledge the human tendency to focus on what you don't have instead of what you do.
- Sing a new song of praise as you recount the wonderful things God has done for you.
- Desire an openness that immediately recognizes and willingly receives God's mercies.

GOD'S REMEDY FOR SIN

We have been justified through faith.

ROMANS 5:1

Paul looked with intrepid eyes into the darkness of the world; but he looked upon it with eyes lit with hope. He knew that God's remedy for sin was full, and met all the need. The whole provision was found in Christ. Paul wrote from the standpoint of conviction that the only solution of human problems must come through Christ, that there could be no staunching of humanity's wounds save in the blood that he shed, that there could be no hope for newness of life and the realization of ideals but in living relationship with him.

G. CAMPBELL MORGAN

AS YOU PRAY TODAY:

- Praise God for the blessing of righteousness through faith in Christ.
- Rejoice in the restored fellowship that accompanies this blessing.
- Thank him for your access to his grace and glory because of Christ's work on the cross.

GOOD GUIDANCE

O LORD, you will lead the people you have redeemed.

EXODUS 15:13

When children are small the lessons they must learn seem never ending. Once they master walking, they must learn to run. Buttoning buttons and tying shoes are needed skills, too. But one lesson that children must learn repeatedly is the lesson of obedience. "Hold my hand." "Look at this!" "Stop!" Following these simple commands shows young ones the value of obedience. And when God says, "Follow me! Look at this! Let's go this way!" their experience of obeying your good guidance will make following God's guidance easier, too.

S.M.H.

AS YOU PRAY TODAY:

- Ask God to give you good guidance to share with the little children in your life.
- Intercede for these young ones that their hearts will be open to God's leading in their lives.
- Pray that you will be a good example of following God's leading in your own decisions.

YOUTH DIRECTORS

I noticed among the young men,
a youth who lacked judgment.

PROVERBS 7:7

A poster in a college dormitory proclaimed: "Our youths love luxury. They have bad manners, contempt for authority. They show disrespect for their elders and love to chatter in place of exercise. They no longer rise when their elders enter the room. They contradict their parents, chatter before company, gobble up food, and tyrannize teachers." The author of this apt description? Socrates, in 400 BC!

Young people haven't changed that much over the centuries. And youth directors who share God's good news with them must embody the patience of Job, the wisdom of Solomon, and the courage of David. They need your prayers!

S.M.H.

AS YOU PRAY TODAY:

- Thank God for the youth in your church.
- Praise him for those who minister to young people in your congregation.
- Ask God for creativity, encouragement, energy, and understanding for those who work with this age group.

C-SPAN COMMANDMENTS

I urge . . . that requests, prayers, intercession and thanksgiving be made for everyone—for kings and all those in authority, that we may live peaceful and quiet lives in all godliness and holiness.

1 TIMOTHY 2:1–2

In school a teen was learning how legislators compose bills and how those bills become laws. The whole process seemed daunting, and the teen complained, "It's a good thing God gave his laws on Mt. Sinai, 'cause Moses never would have gotten the Ten Commandments through Washington without a sub-committee study, a bipartisan amendment, or a stint on C-Span!"

It takes a lot to put together our system of government. To devise godly "C-Span commandments," our legislators need our prayers.

S.M.H.

AS YOU PRAY TODAY:

- Bring each of your congress men and women to God's throne.
- Pray for a listening ear that responds quickly and effectively to constituents' concerns.

NAMIBIA'S LIFELINE

Outwardly we are wasting away, yet inwardly we are being renewed day by day.

2 CORINTHIANS 4:16

Imagine a country of 1.6 million people. Imagine that its people speak 21 different languages and are led by a government sympathetic to Christianity. Imagine a Christian radio broadcast that reaches 95 percent of its people. Yet this is only a partial picture of Namibia.

Imagine a cultural climate of alcohol abuse and illiteracy. Imagine that in only ten years, half of the nation will die of AIDS-related illnesses. Namibia needs a lifeline. Namibia needs God's touch.

JESSICA RODRIQUEZ

AS YOU PRAY TODAY:

- Pray for God's truth to touch the people of Namibia and fill them with hope.
- Intercede for those who bring messages of God's love to those stricken with AIDS.
- Pray that the radio messages of sexual purity will touch the hearts of young people and spare them from the ravages of disease.

GOD IS LOVE

The God of love and peace will be with you.

2 CORINTHIANS 13:11

It would not take twenty-four hours to make the world come to God if you could just make people believe that God is love. If you can really make a man believe you love him, you have won him; and if I could only make people really believe that God loves them, what a rush we would see for the kingdom of God! Oh, how they would rush in! Is there a poor wanderer here who has wandered far from Christ? I don't care how sinful you are; let this text sink deep into your soul today, "God is love."

DWIGHT L. MOODY

AS YOU PRAY TODAY:

- Remember that God's love is unchangeable and unfailing.
- Hear his voice of love and compassion whenever he speaks to you.
- Let God's love keep you strong in your love for others.

A HEAVENLY PASSPORT

You are no longer foreigners and aliens, but fellow citizens with God's people.

EPHESIANS 2:19

As a child of missionary parents, he held a unique position. His mother was American, so her nationality was also his. His father was Columbian, so he acquired citizenship from that nation, too. And he was born in Ecuador, so a third passport was granted because of his place of residence at birth. Yet the Bible says that no matter how many passports we hold on earth, we are also citizens of God's kingdom. As children born of God, we hold a heavenly passport. That citizenship supercedes all others. Hallelujah!

S.M.H.

AS YOU PRAY TODAY:

- Thank God for the nation of your birth and citizenship on this planet.
- Rejoice that you have a heavenly passport, too.
- Ask God to show you ways to be a better citizen of each kingdom.

FOLLOW ME

Jesus said, "My sheep listen to my voice;
I know them, and they follow me."

John 10:27

A mother duck and her babies tried to cross a busy street. Cars stopped to let them pass, but halfway across the road, the last duckling stopped, refusing to budge. The mother duck pushed the other babies to safety and hurried back into the road, quacking and urging the duckling to follow her. When she finally reached the duckling, she nudged it with her beak and quacked once more. This time the baby responded. It opened its heart to the mother's "follow me" message and found safety in the tall grass beside the street.

S.M.H.

AS YOU PRAY TODAY:

- Recall those family members who need to respond to Christ's message to follow him.
- Pray that God will keep calling to those loved ones until they find safety in salvation.
- Ask God to show you ways to reinforce his love for them.

MUSIC'S MINISTRY

Worship the L*ORD with gladness;*
come before him with joyful songs.

Psalm 100:2

In a cracked soprano, the old woman sang along with a well-worn tape, smiling and remembering the church service the recording preserved. "My husband had just lost his job," she said as she continued to listen. "I was scared and confused. But then Pastor Grant, our choir director, asked us to sing, "There Is Joy in the Lord." And, oh, that song just chased the cobwebs of fear away. When I told Pastor Grant how much the song meant to me, he said, 'God led me to sing that hymn today. I just *knew* someone needed to hear it.' Oh, how right he was!"

S.M.H.

AS YOU PRAY TODAY:

- Thank God for the music ministers in your church.
- Lift to God the decisions about the music that will be sung and heard in your church.
- Ask God to provide creativity, health, and inspiration for your choir director.

OUR PRESIDENT

Obey your leaders and submit to their authority. They keep watch over you as men who must give an account. Obey them so that their work will be a joy, not a burden, for that would be of no advantage to you.

HEBREWS 13:17

Our Father, at this desperate hour in world affairs, we need thee. May thy wisdom and thy power come upon those whom have been entrusted leadership. May the responsibility lie heavily on their hearts, until they are ready to acknowledge their helplessness and turn to thee. Give to them the honesty, the courage, and the moral integrity to confess that they don't know what to do. Only then can they lead us as a nation beyond human wisdom to thee, who alone hast the answer.

PETER MARSHALL, FORMER CHAPLAIN OF THE US SENATE

AS YOU PRAY TODAY:

- Remember our president, petitioning God for his protection, choice of advisors, and ordered priorities.
- Ask God to fill him with courage and strength to stand for righteousness.
- Intercede for God's wisdom for the decisions he must make this day.

IN HIS TIME

I hope to visit you and talk with you face to face.

2 John 12

Pastor John works with an evangelism program in India's six southern states. His non-stop itinerary includes a three-day stay in Mysore where twenty-three people prayed to receive Jesus as their Savior. A weekend youth camp brought ten young people to the Lord. A weeklong outreach brought the message of the Gospel to 125 families.

An email message from this Indian pastor was filled with many such reports, but it also contained a heartfelt plea: "May the Lord, in his time, open the doors for you to come to India that we might minister together."

AS YOU PRAY TODAY:

- "Go" to India in your prayers, remembering the evangelism teams and the people they will meet.
- Pray for India with intercessions for provision and protection for these teams that travel all night on crowded buses to reach their next destination.

EASY ACCESS

"I revealed myself to those who did not ask for me;
I was found by those who did not seek me,"
says the LORD.

ISAIAH 65:1

Left to ourselves, none of us would care about God. But God came to us, not because of, but in spite of the fact that we did not care. He initiated the relationship we share with him. He comes to all despite our inability to see our need for him. And it is because of his coming and seeking for us that our hearts can respond to him. God grants us easy access to his grace—grace that draws us to himself.

S.M.H.

AS YOU PRAY TODAY:

- Thank God for drawing you to himself.
- Ask him to develop your eternal perspective, renewing your mind to his presence with you always.
- Pray for more of his grace so that you might grow in godly character.

SEAL OF PURITY

Having believed, you were marked in him with a seal, the promised Holy Spirit.

EPHESIANS 1:13

In the 1980s, a disgruntled pharmaceutical employee devised a method of injecting harmful chemicals into supposedly sealed containers. People who used the tainted medicines ended up in hospital emergency rooms. Immediately thereafter, drug companies began to use triple-sealed bottles to ensure their products' purity.

In the same way, when we live our lives apart from God, our hearts are tainted by sin. But when we receive Christ, the Holy Spirit seals us up to ensure our heart's purity and holiness until we reach God's kingdom in heaven.

S.M.H.

AS YOU PRAY TODAY:

- Thank God for sealing you and protecting you with his Spirit.
- Petition him to keep you spiritually genuine, unsullied by the temptations of sin.
- Ask God to help you recognize and enjoy the riches freely available to you through Christ.

SOWING AND REAPING

Remember this: Whoever sows sparingly will also reap sparingly, and whoever sows generously will also reap generously.

2 CORINTHIANS 9:6

The Bible promises that following God's ways will bring us a deep peace that will guard our hearts and minds and reassure us of God's presence (Philippians 4:7–8). What a wonderful promise to apply to our relationships with friends and family, too. Following God's ways by striving for unity, love, and the things that make for peace will help us establish fulfilling, uplifting relationships with others. By sowing the good things of God, we will reap a peaceful influence in our relationships.

S.M.H.

AS YOU PRAY TODAY:

- Search your heart to discover what influence you have on your friends. Is it a good one?
- Pray that God will help you follow his ways in your relationships.
- Ask God to help you live in peace with those who have brought you trouble this past year.

GOIN' AND DOIN'

We are God's workmanship, created in Christ Jesus to do good works, which God prepared in advance for us to do.

EPHESIANS 2:10

Teddy watched his father climb into a neighbor's pickup truck and head to town. Today was moving day for the Smith family. Daddy Frank was going to help. Mama Rose said that Daddy Frank was a good deacon, always "goin' and doin' for God." Daddy Frank distributed food baskets to folks in town and delivered Miss Marie to her doctors' appointments. He kept the church van running and picked up the church bulletins that were left in the pews after Sunday services. Teddy smiled as the truck disappeared around the corner. "When I grow up," he whispered, "I want to be a deacon, just like my Daddy Frank."

S.M.H.

AS YOU PRAY TODAY:

- Thankfully remember the deacons in your church. Name them by name.
- Ask God to give them direction and wisdom in the fulfillment of their duties.

GOD ESTABLISHES

The authorities that exist have been established by God.

ROMANS 13:1

The presidential election proceedings for 2000 will soon be recorded in American history books. Students in later generations will learn all about "chads" and "recounts" and the political maneuvering and legal wrangling that surrounded the selection and certification of the 43rd President of the United States. Yet the words of Mae Harwood, a 93-year-old woman from central New Jersey, should also appear in those history books. During an exit poll Mae said, "I always vote. Sometimes my fellow wins; sometimes the other guy does. But this election will turn out right, 'cause God chooses a winner every time."

S.M.H.

AS YOU PRAY TODAY:

- Ask God to provide honest, concerned citizens to serve as election officials.
- Thank God for the freedoms we have in our country—to vote, to speak, and to pursue life, liberty, and happiness.

A GREAT LEAP FORWARD?

On God we have set our hope that he will continue to deliver us, as you help us by your prayers.

2 CORINTHIANS 1:10–11

In the late 1950s, Chairman Mao Zedong declared a "great leap forward" for China's people as he purged his country of anything that would point to religion, leaving millions of his countrymen dead or victimized. Today China has more Christians in prison or under detention than any other country in the world. Yet the underground church continues to grow. China's house church movement stands on its commitment to preach the Gospel, no matter what the cost.

AS YOU PRAY TODAY:

- Intercede for the continued faithfulness of Chinese pastors and believers.
- Pray for increased access for journalists and businessmen to interior Chinese villages so that anti-religious atrocities can be documented.
- Pray for strength and encouragement for the families of imprisoned pastors.

GOD UNDERSTANDS ME

The Lord knows the thoughts of man.

Psalm 94:11

Who hasn't heard a teenager cry, "You don't understand me!"? We all want to be understood. We want others to comprehend our viewpoint and motivation, our wants and needs, for by understanding these things, maybe people will better appreciate us as individuals.

We don't have to go to all of that trouble with God. Psalm 139 assures us that God already understands us. He made us. He knows how we think. We are not a mystery to him. He is familiar with all of our ways. God understands. No matter what. No matter why. He just does.

S.M.H.

AS YOU PRAY TODAY:

- Thank God for the marvelous way he has made you.
- Praise God that he knows all about you and what matters to you.
- Release the cares of your week to him, knowing that he understands your stress, your concerns, your needs.

PRACTICE PRAYING

Jesus went out to a mountainside to pray, and spent the night praying to God.

LUKE 6:12

I write out my prayers every day. Try writing out your prayers once a week at first. If you find it helpful, do it more often. If it cramps your style, find another way that is more effective for you. Whatever helpful disciplines you choose, practice praying Jesus' way. Make your prayers regular, private, sincere, and specific. For the miracle of prayer to begin operating in our lives, we must finally do only one thing: we must pray.

BILL HYBELS

AS YOU PRAY TODAY:

- Recall that God longs to hear from you and has invited you to pray; accept that invitation.
- Remember that God is interested in you and your needs; tell him what burdens your heart.
- Ask him to show you how to live moment by moment in his presence.

GENTLE REMINDERS

This I call to mind and therefore I have hope.
Because of the LORD's great love we are not consumed,
for his compassions never fail. They are new every morning;
great is your faithfulness.

LAMENTATIONS 3:21–23

Some folks keep a journal to record the happenings of the day. Once full, however, these diaries often languish in the bottom of a drawer. Yet, if the writer retrieves one and begins to reread it, the entries may trigger remembrances of God's past faithfulness.

We can be like "journal entries" for our friends when they face tough times. We can remind them of situations where God provided for a special need or protected them from harm. And as we gently remind them of God's blessings, we'll be bringing them another blessing, too . . . a blessing of hope.

S.M.H.

AS YOU PRAY TOAY:

- Reflect on your friends and the blessings that God has bestowed on them.
- Pray that God will give you an opportunity to gently remind them about God's past blessings.

DOUBLE HONOR

The elders who direct the affairs of the church well are worthy of double honor.

1 TIMOTHY 5:17

They attend monthly meetings and discuss the church budget. They pray with the pastor before worship services. They pass the collection plates and serve on committees. They pray with the shut-ins and teach the church education classes. And they sometimes spend more time on their church responsibilities than they do on their own interests and hobbies. These called ones are the elders in your local church. And Paul told Timothy that they were worthy of double honor.

S.M.H.

AS YOU PRAY TODAY:

- Bring the elders in your church to God's throne. Name them by name.
- Recall how they have ministered to you in God's name by fulfilling their responsibilities. Thank God for their faithfulness.
- Ask God to show you how you can show your elders "double honor" with your words, actions, and attitude.

SUPREME JUSTICE

When justice is done, it brings joy to the righteous.

PROVERBS 21:15

America's 2000 presidential election proved more valuable than merely giving the world a greater understanding of our voting process. Americans came to know their Supreme Court justices, too.

A majority of U.S. citizens could not have named more than two or three of the justices of the highest court in our land prior to the 2000 presidential election. But by the time the Electoral College met in December, those statistics had changed. Yet it is sad that it took a crisis to place the names of these judicial officials at the top of so many prayer lists.

S.M.H.

AS YOU PRAY TODAY:

- Lift our Supreme Court justices up to God for health, wisdom, and guidance.
- Pray for their discernment, balance, and spiritual guidance.
- Ask God to grant them each impartiality, integrity, and accountability.

AN ISLAND NATION

The Lord knows how to rescue godly men from trials.

2 PETER 2:9

The country of Indonesia is made up of 13,500 islands. More than 600 languages are spoken in this island nation. But parts of Indonesia are so difficult to reach that some of its island peoples have never heard God's Word.

Communists tried to take over Indonesia in 1965, but were defeated by a large Muslim contingent. Today Indonesia offers limited freedom to Hindus, Buddhists, and Christians, but the Muslim president has destroyed many Christian churches and has severely limited their evangelistic outreach.

AS YOU PRAY TODAY:

- Ask God to help believers in Indonesia share his love with those of other religions.
- Ask God to provide evangelists to bring God's message of salvation to every inhabited island in this nation.
- Pray that the Muslim government will seek peaceable means to resolve religious conflicts.

STILL IN THE BUSINESS

The LORD who forms the mountains, creates the wind . . . the LORD God Almighty is his name.

AMOS 4:13

The evening news often contains reports about earthquakes, hurricanes, or tornadoes. Reporters attribute these climatic changes to warming and cooling trends over the oceans. Though these facts are true, the reporters overlook what a simple shepherd from Tekoa recognized centuries ago. Amos knew who forms the mountains and affects the weather: "The LORD God Almighty is his name."

God is still in the business of creation. And the Almighty God who takes cares of mountains, moves the winds, and keeps the planets in their orbits is still in the business of creating relationships with us, too. Our concerns are as important to him as the earth-shaking events of the evening news.

S.M.H.

AS YOU PRAY TODAY:

- Thank God for his control of creation.
- Praise him for the relationship you share together.
- Claim God's promise that he will reveal his thoughts to you.

UPRAISED HANDS

The blood of Jesus, God's Son, purifies us from all sin.

1 JOHN 1:7

Luke 24:50 tells us that the last thing the disciples saw before Jesus ascended into heaven were Jesus' hands lifted toward them in blessing. His hands still bore the visible signs of the nails. In those hands the disciples could see both pain and blessing—the pain of the cross, but the blessings of forgiveness and sanctification, too. Jesus' hands, lifted in blessing, confirmed his great sacrifice for all. Because his hands had been upraised on the cross, all followers of Christ—past, present and future—can raise their hands in the eternal joy of salvation. Hallelujah!

S.M.H.

AS YOU PRAY TODAY:

- Praise God for the sacrifice of his Son.
- Acknowledge his gift of forgiveness and of making you holy and pure for his service.
- Commit your heart to sharing the joy of your salvation with someone else today.

GOD'S TOUCH

All who touched Jesus were healed.

MARK 6:56

In the middle of the night, Leila awoke with an urgent sense to pray for her friend Eleanor. Immediately Leila responded, praying for God's healing touch for her friend on the mission field. Months later Leila would learn that at that very hour, Eleanor, living in primitive conditions, was struggling with a breech birth. God heard Leila's prayer for her friend and answered it with a healthy baby girl.

S.M.H.

AS YOU PRAY TODAY:

- Ask God to bless your friends and family with his healing touch.
- Request strength and resistance to colds, flu, and minor illnesses in addition to healing from major medical problems.
- Thank God for placing this prayer concern on your heart. Remember to pray whenever and however he directs.

MR. B.

If anyone sets his heart on being an overseer,
he desires a noble task.

1 TIMOTHY 3:1

For decades Mr. B. had been a trustee in the church. He never missed a meeting; he always had an opinion about the budget; and he even disagreed with the pastor on how many programs and projects the church could or should handle.

But no one doubted Mr. B.'s love for the Lord. When he prayed, everyone bowed their heads: "O Life Giver, grant us thoughts that are higher than our own and strength that goes beyond our own strength so that we may follow the ways of love and goodness, the ways of our Lord and Savior Jesus Christ."

S.M.H.

AS YOU PRAY TODAY:

- Pray for wisdom for those who handle the financial responsibilities of your church.
- Ask for God's direction and guidance for your church's budget committee meetings.
- Pray that God will provide your church with leaders who love the Lord deeply.

POLICIES FOR THE PRECIOUS

Sons are a heritage from the LORD,
children a reward from him.

PSALM 127:3

Children are precious to God. They remind us of our innocence and give us hope for the future of our country and our world. Yet how often do we pray for those people who influence our children's lives? Public and private school board members directly influence children by making important decisions that impact their academic life. Though our children may not have direct contact with individual board members, they will come into contact with policies instituted by them, and their lives will be affected because of those policies.

MIKE WILSON

AS YOU PRAY TODAY:

- Ask God to send godly school board members to your school district.
- Pray that God will give discernment about the implications of their policy decisions.
- Ask for God to deter any policies that would lead your school district away from godly principles.

SOLZHENITSYN'S WORLD

Thus far has the LORD helped us.

1 SAMUEL 7:12

Through his many writings, Aleksandr Solzhenitsyn gave the West an insider's look at Siberia under Soviet domination. While the harsh, extreme climatic and living conditions continue, Siberia is experiencing the warmth of the Gospel for the first time. Twenty ethnic groups are scattered throughout Siberia's forests, mountains, and tundra. Most of these groups worship animist spirits or shamans, but a few evangelical congregations have been planted among the Yakut and Evenki by Slavic and Estonian missionaries. Missionaries are also beginning to translate the New Testament into nine of the major Siberian languages.

AS YOU PRAY TODAY:

- Ask God to send hardy, pioneer missionaries to the isolated peoples of Siberia.
- Pray that the translation efforts go swiftly and smoothly.
- Intercede for the opening of Siberian hearts to the knowledge of Christ, beginning with the animist shamans.

STARS AND HEARTACHES

God heals the brokenhearted . . .
He determines the number of the stars.

PSALM 147:3, 4

There is nothing that makes a man feel so tiny and so powerless as the sight of God's myriad worlds—nothing, perhaps, but the heartbreaks of life. We stand silenced before them, utterly powerless to avert or alleviate them. They are as great in their power to teach us our limitations as are the stars. Millions of stars are hidden from our gaze even when we are assisted by the strongest telescopes. How like our heartbreaks! Their causes are often hidden. Their number is incalculable. And it takes the God of the stars to heal our sorrows.

J. STUART HOLDEN

AS YOU PRAY TODAY:

- Rely on the might of God's grace in the midst of your heartache.
- Remember his limitless ability to bring comfort and lasting assurance.
- Reflect on past times when God has helped you through heartache.

NEVER FORSAKEN

God has said: "I will live with them and walk among them."

2 CORINTHIANS 6:16

When blessings seem abundant, the truth of this verse is easy to comprehend. But what about when we face death or illness, lose a job or a spouse, or experience an unkind word or deed? In times like these our faith is tested to solidify our knowledge about God and his work in our lives. Yet we needn't worry about how to face the day. We are never forsaken. God will go with us. We just need to hold his hand and walk in faith.

S.M.H.

AS YOU PRAY TODAY:

- Remember that God specializes in impossibilities. Bring your challenges to his throne.
- See yourself in the midst of your problem. Look closely. Find God there, too. Rejoice in his presence.
- Verbalize your trust in him, and accept his peace. Ask him to guide you through this dark time.

SET AN EXAMPLE

Set an example for the believers in speech, in life, in love, in faith and in purity.

1 TIMOTHY 4:12

In team sports when one member experiences a tough time, the other team members rally around them to encourage them to try harder, do better, and keep going. The team members also work harder, too, recognizing that a good example can cheer a disheartened team member to better performance.

Our friends need this kind of example from us. Following God's guidelines is not always an easy thing to do. But our example may be just the thing to help our friends stay strong in their commitment to follow God.

S.M.H.

AS YOU PRAY TODAY:

- Thank God for your friends and for the privilege of being their example.
- Ask him to help you find ways to encourage your friends in their Christian walk.
- Praise God for his power at work in your lives.

POLISHED THANKS

The body is not made up of one part but of many. . . . God has arranged the parts in the body, every one of them, just as he wanted them to be.

1 CORINTHIANS 12:14, 18

Sara's grandfather was the church custodian. He needed extra help keeping the church clean at Christmas time, so Sara had been drafted to wipe the white pews clean of dirty handprints and boot marks. Sara was grimly polishing the pews after an evening service when Grandpa said quietly, "Every time I push a broom or empty the trash, I thank God for my job. Shouldn't you?" Sara ducked her head, but Grandpa's words had hit their mark. By the time Sara finished polishing the row, she found that she could thank God—even for a job polishing pews.

S.M.H.

AS YOU PRAY TODAY:

- Thank God for the custodians who keep your church neat and clean.
- Pray for your custodian's safety in using electrical equipment, ladders, and grounds-keeping machinery.
- Ask God for a way to show your appreciation to your custodian for keeping things in good order.

MAN'S IDEAL

The LORD raised up judges,
who saved the [people of Israel].

JUDGES 2:16

Circuit court justices set precedents that can influence the interpretation of law for years to come. A former judicial leader prayed: "O God by whom the meek are guided in judgment, and light riseth up in the darkness for the godly; grant us, in all our doubts and uncertainties, the grace to ask what thou wouldst have us do, that the Spirit of Wisdom may save us from all false choices and that in thy light we may see light, and in thy straight path may not stumble."

WILLIAM BRIGHT

AS YOU PRAY TODAY:

- Remember the elected circuit court officials in your jurisdiction. Find their names and pray specifically for each one.
- Pray for the cases that each judge will hear. Intercede for fairness, integrity, and discernment.
- Ask God to grant each judge a clear understanding of law and a respect for God's principles.

RULES AND REGULATIONS

Christ redeemed us from the curse of the law by becoming a curse for us.

GALATIANS 3:13

The Wodaabe and Tuareg peoples of Niger live in fear of taboos and curses. Wodaabe women do not speak to, touch, or mention the names of their first- or second-born children upon curse of death. Wodaabe men never speak about their wives in conversation for the same reason.

Tuareg families believe that jealous looks or words can cause miscarriages. And Tuareg men always cover their faces with veils to protect themselves against night spirits and evil words. These peoples are bound by endless rules and regulations. Both tribes need to find true freedom in Christ.

AS YOU PRAY TODAY:

- Ask God to set the Wodaabe and Tuareg peoples free from the curse of their own taboos.
- Pray that these peoples would hunger for true freedom in Jesus Christ.
- Ask God to send Christians from neighboring countries to demonstrate Christ's freedom in their own lives.

THE ORIGINAL STORYTELLER

I will open my mouth in parables, I will utter hidden things, things from of old—we will tell the next generation the praiseworthy deeds of the LORD, his power, and the wonders he has done.

PSALM 78:2, 4

Do you remember the stories you loved hearing as a child—Mother Goose, Aesop's fables, pioneer adventures, science fiction tales? Even when no one was around, you could revisit a story in your mind, visualizing its details.

The original Storyteller inspired ancient prophets to warn his people with stories of stolen lambs, plumb lines, and boiling cauldrons. Jesus' earthly ministry was filled with stories of sons, coins, seeds, and sparrows. Though these stories confused some, those who listened to them with childlike faith could easily revisit those stories, time and again, and hear the clear message of God's love.

S.M.H.

AS YOU PRAY TODAY:

- Thank God for the stories that have brought you to a closer understanding of him.
- Ask him to help you interpret his other stories recorded in Scripture.
- Pray for an opportunity to share God's stories with others.

CHOSEN BY GOD

God chose us in Christ before the creation of the world.

EPHESIANS 1:4

A journalist reporting the results of an election had to fit his story into a narrow column on the first page. The omission of a comma, however, changed his headline from the political statement *He's Finally Been Chosen, by God!* to a theological declaration *He's Finally Been Chosen by God!* While the reporter may not have been happy with the final result of his headline, as Christians we are pleased that we have been chosen by God to be a part of his family. And who knows, maybe that elected official was, too!

S.M.H.

AS YOU PRAY TODAY:

- Rejoice that God has chosen you to be his child.
- Praise him for the gift of grace and the mercy of forgiveness.
- Thank him for his Son's sacrifice and the promise of eternal life.

PRAY THE BIBLE

"[My word] will not return to me empty,
but will accomplish what I desire
and achieve the purpose for which I sent it," says the Lord.

ISAIAH 55:11

Praying intentionally with Scripture in mind is like choosing to follow a map in new territory. Suddenly we can spot several worthy destinations. We can pray confidently and specifically: "Help Neil to understand that if he'll just acknowledge you as Lord today, you will show him how to solve this problem" (Proverbs 3:6). When we pray the Bible, we speak to God in the words of God with the truth of God.

DAVID KOPP

AS YOU PRAY TODAY:

- Pray the Bible for your loved ones. Go beyond "bless them" to requesting God to contend fiercely with every circumstance and power for their lives (Isaiah 49:25–26).
- Ask God to command his angels to guard your family and friends (Psalm 91:11).
- Thank God that he has promised to be our champion (Isaiah 43:5–7).

HOURLY MIRACLE WORKERS

Respect those who work hard among you. . . . Hold them in the highest regard in love because of their work.

1 THESSALONIANS 5:12–13

A church secretary was once told, "Dearie, you have it easy. All you do is type!" How shortsighted that comment was. Your church secretary probably records the offerings given each week; tracks all births, deaths, marriages, and membership changes; handles the pastor's correspondence; publishes the church's bulletins and newsletters; decorates the bulletin boards; keeps small children amused while their parents are busy; makes coffee; answers telephones; listens to parishioners complaints; sends and receives mail; keeps office equipment repaired; orders church supplies; etc. In short, your church secretary is an hourly miracle worker!

S.M.H.

AS YOU PRAY TODAY:

- Thank God for competent, friendly secretaries who keep your church running smoothly.
- Pray that God will give your church secretary an extra blessing this day.

ALL THAT THEY CAN BE

There were three hundred thousand men ready for military service, able to handle the spear and shield.

2 CHRONICLES 25:5

Recruiting advertisements tout the benefits of serving in the armed forces, yet those who have seen active duty know the hardships that come with armed service. Veterans of past wars made sacrifices that preserved the freedoms we take for granted. Active servicemen and women stand ready to defend us against aggression. Because of their dedication, we can rush about our days without worrying whether the airplanes we hear overhead carry innocent passengers or deadly bombs.

S.M.H.

AS YOU PRAY TODAY:

- Remember all who serve our country in the armed services, ROTC programs, and National Guard units nationwide.
- Thank God for faithful veterans who gave of themselves to guarantee your freedom.
- Ask God to put you in touch with a serviceman or woman. Regularly encourage them with letters, calls, and prayers.

MINING UZBEK GOLD

I will give you the treasures of darkness, riches stored in secret places, so that you may know that I am the LORD.

ISAIAH 45:3

Boasting the world's biggest gold mine, Uzbekistan stands on the edge of affluence. Yet a lack of water hinders economic growth in this central Asian, Marxist country. Totalitarian leadership also hinders the mining of the gold of Uzbek hearts. Influenced by a growing Muslim majority, government officials require church registration for each Christian fellowship. Pastors and church members are routinely threatened and arrested.

AS YOU PRAY TODAY:

- Trust God to bridge the cultural divide between the many ethnic groups residing in Uzbekistan so that dangerous conflicts will not arise.
- Pray for effective, fruitful Christian outreach among the rural Uzbeks where Islam is on the rise.
- Intercede for strength and courage for Uzbek believers as they continue to be a light to those around them who live in darkness.

GOD AND CHILI

The Word became flesh and made his dwelling among us.

JOHN 1:14

A little boy said to his mother, "I'm hungry. My Sunday School teacher talked about God and chili today. She said Jesus was God *con carne*. Can we have chili for lunch, please?"

The boy's ears heard "chili," but his teacher was trying to communicate the miracle of Christ's humanity. No other religion offers such a gift—God himself, in the form of Jesus, left heaven to become flesh and blood, to live on earth. Not *con carne*, but *incarnate*—God with us in the flesh.

S.M.H.

AS YOU PRAY TODAY:

- Thank God for sending his incarnate Son to live, love, and die among us.
- Rejoice that you have a Savior who is familiar with the blessings and shortcomings of life in this world.
- Pray for an increased awareness of God's presence with you as you go about your day.

GOD'S GRIT

I have fought the good fight, I have finished the race, I have kept the faith.

2 TIMOTHY 4:7

In the midst of life and deeds, it is easy to have endurance. But thy Word, O Lord, teaches us that this is not enough to bring good to the world. For *this* we must learn to finish things—to bring them to accomplishment and full fruition. We must not be content with plans, ambitions and resolves, but be set and determined to fulfill the promise and complete the task. Give us then, O God, to resist today the temptation of shirking and the grit to endure to the end. Amen.

WILLIAM E. B. DUBOIS

AS YOU PRAY TODAY:

- Ask God to help you finish those tasks that have fallen prey to procrastination.
- Determine to stand firm in the godly grit of perseverance until you accomplish God's will.
- Pray that God will remove any obstacles that stand in your way.

REGULARLY, EARNESTLY, PERSISTENTLY

You do not have, because you do not ask God.

JAMES 4:2

When was the last time you prayed diligently over a period of time for your spouse, your parents, your children? I've heard it said that if you bring a thimble to God, he'll fill it. If you bring a bucket to God, he'll fill that. If you bring a five-hundred-gallon barrel to God, he'll fill that, too. Are your expecting God to fill your needs? Are you asking him to do so—regularly, earnestly, persistently?

BILL HYBELS

AS YOU PRAY TODAY:

- Thank God for the work he has been doing in your family.
- Commit yourself to a purposeful prayer on behalf of your spouse or children.
- Resolve to pray earnestly for a determined length of time for a specific need in your family's lives.

SHUT IN OR OUT?

[Publius'] father was sick in bed, suffering from fever and dysentery. Paul went in to see him and, after prayer, placed his hands on him and healed him.

ACTS 28:8

Ruthie suffers from myasthenia gravis, a debilitating neurological disease that prevents her from attending church. Though Ruthie's church consistently cares for folks with new babies or post-surgical problems, finding people interested in visiting the chronically or critically ill is difficult. Since Ruthie is confined to her home, the pastor visits as often as possible, yet Ruthie feels shut out of fellowship with her church because of limited contact with other parishioners.

S.M.H.

AS YOU PRAY TODAY:

- Lift the names of church shut-ins to God, interceding for relief from the boredom and loneliness of recuperation and chronic illness.
- Pray for opportunities to minister to your church shut-ins—through a phone call, note, or visit.

MAYBERRY MEMORIES

I have posted watchmen on your walls, . . .
they will never be silent day or night.

ISAIAH 62:6

Andy Griffith and Don Knotts immortalized the escapades of a sheriff and his deputy in a rural town in North Carolina. Though this sitcom painted a rosy picture of police work, in real life our sheriffs, deputies, and police officers must look at life through a filter of danger. Every room they enter is quickly assessed for easy exits or places to take cover. Details that we overlook—hair color, height, license plate number—are top priorities for them. Even off duty, law enforcement personnel stand ready to serve and protect.

S.M.H.

AS YOU PRAY TODAY:

- Intercede for health and safety for community law enforcement personnel.
- Ask God to encourage godly sheriffs, deputies, and officers to bring God's focus back to law enforcement.
- Pray for your police chief and for the officers who patrol your neighborhood. Learn their names and send them a note of thanks.

PAKISTANI PERSEVERANCE

Stand firm and you will see the deliverance the LORD will bring you.

EXODUS 14:13

Pakistan faces a daunting array of social, economic, and ecological problems. Constitutional rights of minorities are being eroded and basic human rights have been ignored for non-Muslim groups, women, and the poor. Persecution of Christians has rapidly increased since 1988, with many Christians being falsely charged with blaspheming Mohammed—a crime punishable by death. Yet Pakistani believers persevere in boldly sharing their love for Christ.

AS YOU PRAY TODAY:

- Pray for a pure testimony for Pakistani believers and for strength, boldness, and courage to share their faith.
- Ask God to move the Pakistani government to make laws that protect human rights.
- Pray that extremist proposals for religious persecution will be defeated in Pakistan's parliament.

THE SHEPHERD

His sheep follow him because they know his voice.

John 10:4

There is an intimate relationship between the Shepherd and the sheep, which is always initiated by the Shepherd himself. But there is something for the sheep to do when he enters the fold. He has to be willing to hear and respond to the Shepherd's voice.

He has long sought you, called to you, prepared for you, loved you. Now you know the way into the fold. Respond to the Shepherd himself: Jesus Christ.

Rosalind Rinker

AS YOU PRAY TODAY:

- Praise God for the privilege of being a member of his flock.
- Picture yourself as a lamb in the safety of your Shepherd's arms. Rest and trust in his care.
- Pray for a clear understanding of the Shepherd's voice. His voice will affirm Scripture, lead to freedom, and glorify God.

GOD'S TIMETABLE

My times are in your hands, O Lord.

Psalm 31:15

Elisha's servant Gehazi was telling the king about a young man that Elisha had restored to life. Just then, the young man's mother arrived in the king's palace requesting a favor. Coincidence? Not hardly. God's timing? Definitely! When we wait for God's timing and then follow his direction, we needn't worry that any of the doors that open to us are beyond God's control. Our times are in God's hands. He will bring us where we need to be when we need to be there. We must only wait and walk according to his timetable.

S.M.H.

AS YOU PRAY TODAY:

- Submit your plans to God's timetable. Let God control your calendar.
- Thank God for the times he has allowed you to be in the right place at the right time.
- Prayerfully ask God to help you wait for his timing in all things.

A MOTHER'S PRAYER

She forgets the anguish because of her joy that a child is born.

JOHN 16:21

Phillis Wheatley was the first African-American woman to become a published author. Her prayer for a mother-to-be was penned in 1779: "O my Gracious Preserver! Be pleased to give me strength to bring forth living and perfect a being who shall be greatly instrumental in promoting thy glory. Thy infinite wisdom can bring a clean thing out of an unclean, a vessel of Honor filled for thy glory. Grant me also the spirit of Prayer and Supplication according to thy own most gracious Promises."

AS YOU PRAY TODAY:

- Remember a pregnant friend or family member. Ask God to grant health and safety to mother and child.
- Ask for God's guidance as she prepares her home, family, and heart for a new life.
- Pray that the new mother will make wise choices, putting the baby's interests ahead of her own.

PERFECT US

Excel in gifts that build up the church.

1 Corinthians 14:12

John Wesley recognized the importance of each believer in the working of the church when he prayed: "As you find pleasure in the prosperity of your servants, so let us take pleasure in the service of our Lord, and find success in your work, and in your love and praise forever. Fill up all that is empty, and change whatever is wrong in us. Let the joy of your pardoning love always stay in all our hearts. Amen."

AS YOU PRAY TODAY:

- Pray for the members of your church congregation. Recall by name the ones who sit near you each week.
- Pray for those in your congregation who are facing personal struggles. Bring those problems to God's throne.
- Pray for those who have just joined your church. Ask God to help you make them feel welcome and needed.

EMERGENCY!

Reach down your hand from on high;
deliver me and rescue me, O Lord.
Psalm 144:7

It's still dark outside when his beeper goes off, but Dave hurries out of bed and shrugs into the clothes that stand ready on the bedpost. Last night's weather forecast, the early timing of this call, and the location of the emergency alert Dave to the probability of finding a bad auto accident with injuries. As a first responder, Dave's presence may mean the difference between life and death for those involved. Emergency medical technicians, ambulance drivers, and first responders are our lifelines for survival at such times.

S.M.H.

AS YOU PRAY TODAY:

- Pray for first responders to have keen eyes and clear minds to administer care and comfort when they arrive on the scene.
- Pray for wisdom and skill for EMTs as they minister healing to accident victims.
- Pray for safety as ambulance drivers speed patients to hospitals and care centers.

A LAND OF TURMOIL

You are a chosen people, a royal priesthood, a holy nation, a people belonging to God, that you may declare the praises of him who called you out of darkness into his wonderful light.

1 PETER 2:9

Iraq has been a troubled land since Bible times, but under the rule of Saddam Hussein the turmoil has increased. A decade of war and hardship brought Iraq to an economic standstill. Saddam Hussein has allowed religious minorities in Iraq provided they demonstrate political loyalty to his views, but the importing of Bibles and Christian literature is severely restricted.

AS YOU PRAY TODAY:

- Pray that Iraqi Christians will find ways to share Jesus' love with others.
- Invoke God's power to bind the evil that broods over Iraq so that people may see the truth of the Gospel.
- Pray specifically for the Marsh Arabs who live by the Tigris River. No known outreach has ever touched this remote Iraqi group.

BEST FRIENDS

There is a friend who sticks closer than a brother.

PROVERBS 18:24

Best friends share secrets and hidden desires. They know what you're thinking and what you're about to say before you say it. They know your likes and dislikes, your favorite colors and foods, your hopes, dreams, and aspirations.

Best friends never lose your address and always know how to get in touch with you. They think of you often, even on vacation. They know everything about you, too, the good and the bad, but they won't tell because they wouldn't want to hurt you.

Are you best friends with God?

S.M.H.

AS YOU PRAY TODAY:

- Thank God for his offer of friendship. Take him up on it.
- Consider how you can be a better friend of God. Trust him to show you.
- Look for ways that you can introduce him to others. Let him be their best friend, too.

DECISIONS, DECISIONS

If any of you lacks wisdom, he should ask God, who gives generously to all without finding fault, and it will be given to him.

JAMES 1:5

From momentous choices to minute ones, we make countless decisions that affect our lives. Lot faced a major decision when he was offered the choice of a homeland. David faced a major decision when the Philistines carried off his family and his men urged quick retaliation. Yet, the outcome of those two decisions was vastly different. Lot depended on his own resources to make his choice and soon found himself headed for disaster. David, however, took time to sit quietly and talk to the Lord. Only then did he make a decision that was both pleasing to God and a blessing to his family.

S.M.H.

AS YOU PRAY TODAY:

- Bring your decisions to God first before making up your mind about them.
- Ask God to remind you of Bible verses that would help in your decision-making.
- Pray that God will clearly confirm the decision you should make.

WELL-TIMED PRAYERS

Pray in the Spirit on all occasions.

EPHESIANS 6:18

A friend went to visit her son and daughter-in-law. When the son didn't return from work, Mom began to feel uneasy. She said, "I'm concerned. Let's drive toward his workplace." They saw him coming from the other direction on his motorcycle. As they watched, he veered off the road, hit the curb and flew 40 feet through the air. As he was moving through the air, Mom was praying, "Jesus, protect my son!" They ran to the scene and found a miracle! No injuries! Does this mean that if you weren't praying when someone had an accident, you're to blame? Of course not. It simply means we must be alert. When warnings come from the Holy Spirit, we must respond by praying.

DUTCH SHEETS

AS YOU PRAY TODAY:

- Bring your loved ones to God and pray protection for them.
- Thank God for allowing you to intervene on your loved one's behalf.

BEAN COUNTERS

Those who have served well gain an excellent standing and great assurance in their faith in Christ Jesus.

1 TIMOTHY 3:13

Churches are not moneymaking enterprises, so handling the finances of a church can be a daunting prospect. Your church treasurer has to responsibly collect and disburse your congregation's offerings and keep an accurate record of every transaction. Church treasurers are often derogatorily referred to as "bean counters," "tight wads," or "misers." However, God views our church treasurers in a different light. He calls them "good stewards," "faithful administrators," and "trustworthy servants."

S.M.H.

AS YOU PRAY TODAY:

- Thank God for your church treasurer.
- Ask God to fill your treasurer with wisdom, understanding, and honesty as he fulfills his duties.
- Pray that God will help you be a giver rather than a grumbler when it comes to your church finances.

THE RED CROSS

You sent me aid again and again when I was in need.

PHILIPPIANS 4:16

In 1864, delegates from 12 nations gathered in Geneva, Switzerland to discuss the treatment of wounded soldiers and the protection of medical personnel and hospitals bearing a white flag with a red cross. Since that time, the International Red Cross has helped alleviate the suffering of wounded soldiers, civilians, and prisoners of war. The IRC also gives aid to victims of floods, earthquakes, epidemics, and famines. The American Red Cross, founded in 1881, expands these humanitarian efforts to include nursing and health care programs, counseling services, and financial assistance to victims of disasters.

S.M.H.

AS YOU PRAY TODAY:

- Thank God for the philanthropic work of the Red Cross.
- Pray for Red Cross volunteers as they deliver food, medicines, and supplies to war-ravaged countries.
- Ask God to give Red Cross directors wisdom as they work with governments to minimize the devastation of natural disasters.

AT THE TOP OF THE WORLD

Jesus said, "Blessed are you when people insult you, persecute you and falsely say all kinds of evil against you because of me. Rejoice and be glad, because great is your reward in heaven."

MATTHEW 5:11–12

In 1950, Tibet lost its independence as a Buddhist nation when Chinese communists conquered the land. Since that time the Chinese have invaded every aspect of this nation at the top of the world, destroying its culture and religion. Many Tibetans have been forced into exile. Thousands have been killed because of their faith in Buddha, and the handful of Christians in Tibet today face severe persecution from the government and from faithful Buddhists.

AS YOU PRAY TODAY:

- Pray that God will strengthen the believers in this mountainous nation and bring many Tibetans to Christ.
- Pray that the present sufferings of all religious groups will be the start of a great spiritual awakening to faith in Christ.

AWESOME AND UNDEFINED

How great is God—beyond our understanding!

Job 36:26

My God cannot be chained as a Prisoner of logic or delivered into the custody of a theological proposition. Shame on those who have given him a setting within the points of the compass. For myself, I have a joy wider than knowledge, a conception that domes itself above my best thinking. God! Best defined when undefined; a Life too great for shape or image; a Love for which there is no equal name. Who is he? God. What is he? God. He is at once the question and the answer, the self-balance, the all.

Joseph Parker

AS YOU PRAY TODAY:

- Reflect on your view of God—is it limited or limitless?
- Surround yourself in God, aware of his presence with you, working through you.
- Thank him for the opportunity to see his strength working on your behalf.

THE RIGHT WORD

The word of God is living and active.

HEBREWS 4:12

The Bible is God's actual, living Word. God speaks to us in our day-to-day experiences through the Bible. We can learn truths about God and his character from the Bible. We can be corrected when we are wrong through his living Word. We can be prepared to follow him more closely and find a new path when we have strayed. God will speak the right word to us at the right time through the Bible. We need only take the time to read and listen to his Word. Have you spent time with God's Word today?

S.M.H.

AS YOU PRAY TODAY:

- Commit yourself to a regular time of studying God's Word.
- Ask God to make at least one verse come alive to you when you read his Word.
- Pray for understanding for the things you read in his Word.

FIELDWORK

Jesus said, "The harvest is plentiful but the workers are few. Ask the Lord of the harvest, therefore, to send out workers into his harvest field."

MATTHEW 9:37–38

Fieldwork is physically demanding. Farmers toil year round to bring in their crops. And when farmers retire, younger members often step in to continue their work.

There are sowers and harvesters in God's fields, too. Members of God's fieldwork never retire, but sometimes they move on to new assignments. If we model an example of one who is willing to fill the gap left by other fieldworkers, perhaps others will acquire a servant's heart that is willing to go where God leads and help do whatever God wants. Workers are always needed. Is God calling you to fill a gap left by another?

S.M.H.

AS YOU PRAY TODAY:

- Ask God to show you a fieldwork gap you can fill.
- Call upon God to give you a servant's heart and example that others can follow.
- Pray that God will give you teachable moments to talk to your family about serving others.

CEMETERY TRAINING

Wisdom will enter your heart,
and knowledge will be pleasant to your soul.

PROVERBS 2:10

Seminary professors routinely challenge students' long-held beliefs. Those students who survive their seminary years often bury their misconceptions in the cemetery of seminary and rediscover their love for God mainly because of their professors' repeated hammerings. Reverend John Henry Jowett recognized the importance of seminary professors' training on young minds when he prayed: "Father, teach us not only thy will, but how to do it. Teach us the best way of doing the best thing, lest we spoil the end by unworthy means."

AS YOU PRAY TODAY:

- Remember those professors who will be training future pastors.
- Ask God to grant them wisdom in communicating the truths of Scripture to young minds.
- Pray for encouragement and clarity of thought as seminarians dig through musty volumes to find the vibrant, life-changing truths of God.

POLICIES PENDING

Who can speak and have it happen if the Lord has not decreed it?

LAMENTATIONS 3:37

With the advent of cable television, Americans can receive daily broadcasts from the floor of the United States Congress. At any given time viewers can listen to debates, speeches, and roll call votes on both major and minor policies pending before Congress. Yet the Bible reminds us that God is ultimately in charge of the policies that affect our country. He alone directs the outcome of votes and the balance of power.

S.M.H.

AS YOU PRAY TODAY:

- Lift your senators to God's throne for wisdom and guidance as they deliberate and decide the issues before them.
- Remember your congressmen and women. Pray that they will make Christian principles a priority in their decisions.
- Ask for God's mercy concerning the policies pending in Congress, that he might hinder those that would not be for our good.

SPRINKLED CLEAN

Let us draw near to God with a sincere heart in full assurance of faith, having our hearts sprinkled to cleanse us from a guilty conscience and having our bodies washed with pure water.

HEBREWS 10:22

With only one percent of its population claiming an affiliation with Christianity, Thailand is a nation bound by corruption. Government officials promote drug cartels, crime syndicates, and a large sex industry. The people of Thailand adhere to a complex blend of occult practices, spirit worship, and Buddhism. At the beginning of every year, many Thai families sprinkle water over each family member, believing that the water will wash away the sins of the last year and protect against potential disasters in the year to come.

AS YOU PRAY TODAY:

- Join Thai Christians in praying for a spiritual breakthrough for their nation.
- Pray that honest leaders will be found to stop corruption and lay the foundations for a just society.
- Pray for missionaries in Thailand who must learn two difficult languages in order to share the Gospel message.

DADDY

God sent the Spirit of his Son into our hearts, the Spirit who calls out, "Abba, Father."

GALATIANS 4:6

Abba and *imma*—daddy and mommy—are the first words Jewish children learn to speak. And *abba* is so personal, so familiar a term that no one ever dared to use it in address to the great God of the universe—no one until Jesus. This reality of deepest intimacy permeated everything Jesus said and did. Experientially we are invited into the same intimacy with Father God that he knew while here in the flesh. We are encouraged to crawl into the Father's lap and receive his love and comfort and healing and strength.

RICHARD FOSTER

AS YOU PRAY TODAY:

- Take time in your prayers to laugh and weep, freely and openly, with your *Abba*, Father.
- Feel his presence wrapped around you like a comforting hug.
- Worship his greatness, deep within your spirit.

FAITH-FILLED FINANCES

Whoever trusts in his riches will fall,
but the righteous will thrive.

PROVERBS 11:28

The movie classic "It's a Wonderful Life" contrasts the life of wealthy miser Henry Potter with struggling businessman George Bailey. Bailey invests his life and money in the townspeople and earns their love—a love that Potter could never buy.

God wants us to use our money wisely, too. When facing money woes, we should depend on God to supply our need. And in times of financial abundance, we also need to depend on God to help us share our surplus. With faith-filled finances we will never be isolated like Mr. Potter but will instead watch our finances draw us closer to God and others.

S.M.H.

AS YOU PRAY TODAY:

- Thank God for supplying your needs.
- Ask God to give you wisdom in budgeting and purchases.
- Commit all of your money to God—the surpluses and the shortfalls.

PRAISEWORTHY PRIORITIES

[Hezekiah] sought his God and worked wholeheartedly. And so he prospered.

2 CHRONICLES 31:21

If we want our children to succeed, Hezekiah's priorities should be their priorities, too. It takes constant prioritizing to make sure that God is number one in children's lives. How careful are they to frame their lives with prayer, to build their foundations on God's Word? How careful are we to model these priorities, too?

Hezekiah "worked wholeheartedly." Do our children work hard at anything besides video games? Do they have responsibilities that are appropriate for their age and ability? Do we hold them accountable for these tasks? If our children follow Hezekiah's praiseworthy priorities, they will prosper as he did.

S.M.H.

AS YOU PRAY TODAY:

- Ask God to help you straighten out your children's priorities.
- Pray for ways to help your children develop a time of prayer and Bible study.
- Ask God to help motivate your children to do their schoolwork and chores wholeheartedly.

THOSE WHO CARE, TEACH

When Jesus landed [on the shore] and saw a large crowd, he had compassion on them, because they were like sheep without a shepherd. So he began teaching them many things.

MARK 6:34

People who have been instructed about the kingdom of heaven have in their hearts a storeroom of fresh new insights as well as the time-tested wisdom of the ages. Like hospitable homeowners who share their belongings both old and new, effective teachers refresh others both with wisdom gained in the past and lessons gained through current study and experience.

DR. WALTER CROW

AS YOU PRAY TODAY:

- Pray for God to lead godly men and women into positions as teachers and professors in our universities and colleges.
- Thank God for the refreshment you have been given through the ministry of Bible teachers in your church and community.
- Pray that God will give teachers wisdom on ways to impart the fresh insights he has given them.

POTHOLED PAVEMENTS

Prepare the way for the people. Build up, build up the highway! Remove the stones.

ISAIAH 62:10

A narrow highway winds through mountain passes on its way to several Andean villages. Passengers on crowded buses bump and jostle their way down the road. Large potholes appear around blind curves—some large enough to swallow the front end of a pickup truck. The seventy-mile journey on this South American highway takes almost three hours because of the potholed pavements.

In the United States we take our highways for granted and rarely give much thought to the workers who maintain them. Without their skill and dedication, our roadways would look, and feel, like those Andean mountain roads.

S.M.H.

AS YOU PRAY TODAY:

- Thank God for the comforts of our roadways.
- Pray for the safety of road crews as they maintain our highways.
- Ask God to remind you to drive more carefully in road construction zones.

THE CROSSROADS

Stand at the crossroads and look; ask for the ancient paths, ask where the good way is, and walk in it.

JEREMIAH 6:16

Dry and mountainous, Afghanistan has been called "the Crossroads of Central Asia." Its central location has brought problems, however. For centuries Afghanistan has struggled with invaders. Extremist Muslims overthrew Afghanistan's Communist government in 1992, inciting a holy civil war for religious and political supremacy. Though Christian relief workers are welcomed, missionaries are forbidden. Outsiders who share their faith are punished, and an open profession of Christ for an Afghan means a death sentence.

AS YOU PRAY TODAY:

- Pray for the eighty-eight unreached people groups in Afghanistan. May the light of the Gospel penetrate their spiritual darkness.
- Pray for openness to the Gospel among Afghans who question the brutality of Islamic leaders.
- Pray for strength, provision, and protection for the handful of believers who courageously share their faith.

A RIGHTEOUS SAVIOR

I, with a song of thanksgiving, will sacrifice to you. What I have vowed I will make good. Salvation comes from the LORD.

JONAH 2:9

The Bible tells us that after a three-day stay in the belly of a great fish, God delivered Jonah from his disobedience and set him on a path of submission. Jonah had run from God, embarking via a cargo boat from the shores of self-will, but God deposited him on the sands of relinquishment. His spirit of contention was replaced with a sense of commitment. His heart of stone was broken with the oil of gladness. Truly, salvation comes from a righteous God.

S.M.H.

AS YOU PRAY TODAY:

- Lay your life before God and declare your intent to follow his will.
- Confess your self-sufficiency and struggles with submission and surrender.
- Pray for a heart that is free from prejudices that can limit your faithfulness to God.

WITH HEAD AND HEART

Love the L*ORD your God with all your heart and with all your soul and with all your strength.*

DEUTERONOMY 6:5

We often go through the motions of worship with our heads, but never let our hearts into the process. We sit and sing the hymns during worship services, but our hearts are concerned with paying the dentist bill or handling a problem with our in-laws.

To truly worship God we need our heads and our hearts. We must clear our minds of the mundane worries that plague us and respond to God by recognizing the wonders of his person and experiencing the truths he shows us about himself. Only then will we be able to worship God "in spirit and in truth" (John 4:24).

S.M.H.

AS YOU PRAY TODAY:

- Consider God's power in and around you—in your life, in creation, in others.
- Thank God for his provision for your daily needs.
- Ask God how you should respond to what you are learning about him.

A TEACHER'S PRAYER

Those who are wise will instruct many.

DANIEL 11:33

In the 1840s, Ann Plato taught African-American children in Hartford, CT. Her prayers for God's direction and inspiration in her teaching resound in this poem:

While I strive to govern human heart,
May I the heavenly precepts still impart;
Oh! May each youthful bosom catch the sacred fire,
And youthful mind to virtue's throne aspire . . .
Oh, grant me active days of peace and truth,
Strength to my heart, and wisdom to my youth,
A sphere of usefulness—a soul to fill
That sphere with duty, and perform thy will.

AS YOU PRAY TODAY:

- Remember the teachers who have a direct influence on your children. Name them by name.
- Intercede for God to give each one direction and inspiration in their teaching this week.
- Ask God to surround each classroom with peace and freedom from distraction and disruption from troublemakers.

GOING WITH GOD

The LORD will watch over your coming and going both now and forevermore.

PSALM 121:8

How wonderful to rest and spend more time with family and friends. A vacation gives us the means to enjoy more of God's bounty. But we are not the only ones who need a time away from our regular routines. Our pastors need that time of refreshing, too.

Our pastors need time to find God in the quiet of a sunrise, the laughter of children, the smile of a spouse or relative. Their vacation isn't a time away *from* God, but rather a time to reconnect *with* God, sensing his presence and care for them.

S.M.H.

AS YOU PRAY TODAY:

- Intercede for your pastors as they face the pressures of this week.
- Pray that God will help your pastors schedule vacations—and take them.
- Thank God for bringing your pastor closer to him through this time of relaxation.

A GREAT SANDWICH

You will eat the fruit of your labor;
blessings and prosperity will be yours.

Psalm 128:2

Henry makes a great Syrian sandwich! When his delicatessen doors open every day, the aromas that waft onto the sidewalk are tantalizing. Yes, Henry works hard, but so do all the small business owners in your community. Without your patronage, small businesses wouldn't be able to pay their bills and stay open. Their storefronts would be vacant, inviting vandalism, and bringing property values down. Encourage the business owners that provide good service to your community. Get to know them. Frequent their establishments. And pray for them.

S.M.H.

AS YOU PRAY TODAY:

- Single out a business that is close to your home. Get to know the owners and pray for them.
- Ask God to send many customers to this establishment to help keep this store in the black.
- Pray that God will bring good tenants to your neighborhood's vacant storefronts.

SENEGAL SKILL

My mouth will tell of your righteousness, of your salvation all day long, though I know not its measure. I will come and proclaim your mighty acts, O Sovereign LORD; I will proclaim your righteousness, yours alone.

PSALM 71:15–16

Many Christians in Senegal do not follow a Christian lifestyle. In fact, the large Muslim population refers to Christians as "those who drink" rather than those who follow Christ. Some of these Muslims are members of the Wolof tribe. Despite concerted efforts by missionaries, these proud people have been resistant to the Gospel and still use charms and consult spirits. Yet the Wolof respect those who speak with skill and wisdom, and urge their children to develop their verbal skills through storytelling.

AS YOU PRAY TODAY:

- Pray that missionaries would find ways to share Jesus' stories to reach the people of Senegal.
- Intercede for safety for missionaries living among hostile, Muslim factions.

THREE TIMES TRUTHFUL

God is truthful.

John 3:33

Telling the truth is so important to our justice system that a person must place their hand on a Bible and swear before God and all present that the words spoken by them in court will be truthful. Why is truth so important? Truth removes the possibility of error or bias. And truth forces us to view ourselves in the light of God's character. John 3:33 says that God is truth; 1 John 5:6 says that the Holy Spirit is truth; and Jesus calls himself truth in John 14:6. Three times in John's writings, God's Word declares truth to be an integral part of his character.

S.M.H.

AS YOU PRAY TODAY:

- Ask God to search your heart. Are you truthful in all your ways?
- Ask God to cleanse your spirit. Repent of thoughts and words that are less than truthful.
- Ask God to enlighten your mind. Study what the Bible has to say about truth.

KEEP PRAYING

The prayer offered in faith will make the sick person well.

JAMES 5:15

Despite the repeated prayers of family and friends, a woman was unable to move her legs, paralyzed by an unknown virus. One evening while the household slept, a burglar entered a downstairs room adjacent to the woman's bedroom. Hearing noises in the night and recognizing that they came from a burglar and not a family member so terrified the woman that she leapt out of bed and ran to the stairway to call for help. Doctors said the reversal of her paralysis could only be deemed a miracle.

S.M.H.

AS YOU PRAY TODAY:

- Remember that God is a God of miracles.
- Bring your health concerns to him, knowing that he hears and cares about every prayer.
- Trust God to bring about his best for your healing—whether through conventional medicine or through miraculous means—and in his time.

FAMILY FRICTION

Forgive as the Lord forgave you.

COLOSSIANS 3:13

When a family member insults us, our immediate response is not usually charitable. We may return an insult in kind or become defensive. Yet a more healing response would contain love and forgiveness.

When we put love into the equation for dealing with hurt, we can look past the act or insult and see another's needs. We may find that we have done something that could have been misinterpreted. We may have made an error that inadvertently hurt them first. And our own error may make the insult we've suffered not look so bad. Let's love and forgive first to heal family friction fast.

S.M.H.

AS YOU PRAY TODAY:

- Bring your hurts and slights to the Father.
- Ask him to help you forgive the family member who said or did these things to you.
- Pray that God will show you a way to love and forgive that person.

SINGING FOR THE SAVIOR

I will sing your praise, O Lord.

PSALM 138:1

Gospel singer Sandi Patti began her singing career as part of her family's singing group. The Patti family—father, mother, Sandi, and two younger brothers—toured the country, singing in church services, camp meetings, and evangelistic crusades. Sandi went on to sing with The Gaither Trio for a year before branching out on her own in the mid-1980s. Sandi Patti, and other Gospel singers like her, fulfill the Psalmist's goal to sing God's praise.

AS YOU PRAY TODAY:

- Pray for Christian musicians that God will inspire them as they minister in his name.
- Intercede for a favorite Gospel singer. Pray for them the same things you would want someone to pray for you.
- Ask God to strengthen Christian musicians who must travel far from home. Give them good rest, good friends, and a good witness.

A COMMUNITY PRAYER

Blessed is the nation whose God is the LORD,
the people he chose for his inheritance.

PSALM 33:12

From war, bloodshed, and violence; from corrupt and unjust government; from sedition and treason: ***Lord, deliver us.***

Raise up those who fall and strengthen those who stand; comfort and help the fainthearted and the distressed: ***Gracious Lord, help us.***

Give all nations justice and peace; preserve our country from discord and strife; direct and guard those who have civil authority; bless and guide all our people: ***Dear Lord, hear us.***

Reconcile us to our enemies, persecutors, and slanderers; help us use wisely the fruits and treasure of the earth, the sea, and the air: ***Graciously hear our prayers.***

AS YOU PRAY TODAY:

- Thank God for the freedom you have to pray and worship in public.
- Intercede for God's mercy in directing the affairs of our nation.

A CORAL VOID

Open their eyes and turn them from darkness to light, and from the power of Satan to God.

ACTS 26:18

Twelve hundred coral islands in the Indian Ocean make up the Republic of Maldives, the least evangelized nation in the world. No resident missionaries have ever been allowed in Maldives. There are no known Maldivian Christians because the government enforces total allegiance to Islam. No Bibles or Christian literature may be legally imported, and all known Christian foreigners were expelled from the country in 1998.

AS YOU PRAY TODAY:

- Ask God to open unique media opportunities for bringing the Gospel to Maldives.
- Pray that God will fill the void left by the removal of foreign Christians through Christian tourists and fishermen who trade with the Maldivians.
- Ask God to send Maldivian students and workers into other countries so that they may learn about Christ, believe in him, return home, and share their faith.

WHAT MORE THAN GRACE?

You, O Lord, are a compassionate and gracious God.

Psalm 86:15

The gracious gifts of God stand every day before your eyes whichever way you look: father and mother, house and homestead, peace, safety, and security through worldly government, etc. Over and above all this he gave his beloved Son for you and through his Gospel brought him home to you, to help you in every grief and dire affliction. What more could he have done for you or what more or better could you wish?

Martin Luther

AS YOU PRAY TODAY:

- Thank God for his compassion and kindness that will never fail you.
- Rejoice in the gracious gifts that God bestows on you.
- Commit to take these thoughts to heart and to share them with others.

ARE YOU FROM HEAVEN?

We are therefore Christ's ambassadors, as though God were making his appeal through us.

2 CORINTHIANS 5:20

Chattering in baby-talk gibberish, two little girls sat beside the fountain that surrounded the openwork globe at the entrance to the 1963 World's Fair in Flushing Meadows, NY. A stranger approached and asked them if they were from Norway. The girls giggled in response, but shook their heads. "No, sir," the braver child answered, "we're from Philadelphia!"

The stranger's mistake was understandable. Everything about the girls' appearance suggested they were representatives from a foreign land. Is there enough of Christ's likeness showing through our lives that a casual stranger would assume we belonged to the kingdom of heaven?

S.M.H.

AS YOU PRAY TODAY:

- Thank God for the opportunity to be his ambassador.
- Ask him to help you more accurately reflect his kingdom in your words and ways.
- Pray for an opening to speak to someone else about your heavenly home.

DEMOLISHING DARKNESS

Though we live in the world, we do not wage war as the world does. The weapons we fight with are not the weapons of the world. On the contrary, they have divine power to demolish strongholds.

2 Corinthians 10:3–4

I saw a huge building demolished several years ago. The demolition crew used dynamite, strategically placed by experts to demolish this major structure in less than ten seconds. This in some ways can also be a picture of our intercession. Unlike this physical building, we don't usually see the answer in seconds—we may be strategically placing the dynamite of the Spirit for days, weeks, or months. But sooner or later there will be a mighty explosion in the spirit, a stronghold will crumble to the ground and a person will fall to their knees.

Dutch Sheets

AS YOU PRAY TODAY:

- Intercede for protection for the lost members of your family.
- Ask God to put godly people in their path each day.
- Pray for God's enlightenment to show these loved ones their need for Christ.

REACH OUT WITH OUTREACH

Jesus said, "As the Father has sent me, I am sending you."

JOHN 20:21

Churches offer outreach programs for young children and teens. Though some argue that such programs are nothing more than entertainments, these outreach efforts present God's message in nonthreatening ways. A Sunday School teacher who uses games to reinforce her lessons once heard a child tell her mother, "We played a game with Mrs. Pike today. I learned all the books in the Bible, and I didn't even mean to!" Mrs. Pike's ingenuity reached one small child. God expects all of us to use what he has given us, too, to reach out and teach our children.

S.M.H.

AS YOU PRAY TODAY:

- Ask God to give you vibrant, new ideas to reach children with the Gospel.
- Pray for programs and outreach opportunities in your church and community.
- Search your heart for a willingness to be of service in these outreach ministries to children and teens.

FIRE!

God will command his angels concerning you
to guard you in all your ways.

PSALM 91:11

A piercing cry shattered the darkness: "My car's on fire!" By the time the young mother secured her children, fire crews were already on the scene, training their equipment on the burning vehicle to keep the gas tank from exploding. Then, with expert precision, they quickly dispatched secondary blazes that threatened the neighbor's porch and the young mother's garage. When the fires were out, the young mother sobbed to the fire crew, "What would we have done without you?"

S.M.H.

AS YOU PRAY TODAY:

- Thank God for the fire department that serves your community. Pray for their protection as they work to protect you.
- Ask God to give your fire crew good health and the strength needed for their job.

BRIDGING TWO CONTINENTS

Who shall separate us from the love of Christ? Shall trouble or hardship or persecution or famine or nakedness or danger or sword? . . . No, in all these things we are more than conquerors through God who loved us.

ROMANS 8:35, 37

Bridging the two continents of Europe and Asia, Turkey is a stronghold of the Muslim faith. Though the law does not forbid freedom of religion to Turkey's citizens, some Turks who have become Christians have lost their jobs and been imprisoned. Because of this, there has been a rapid decline in the number of Christian converts. Christian witness is primarily confined to foreign businessmen and national minorities where growth in fellowship groups is most notable.

AS YOU PRAY TODAY:

- Praise God for his involvement in Turkey and in the lives of Turkish believers.
- Pray for an outpouring of revival through the spread of Christian literature and radio broadcasts.
- Pray that God will replace unrighteous governmental officials with leaders who are sympathetic to the Gospel.

THE LOVER OF OUR SOULS

You are forgiving and good, O Lord,
abounding in love to all who call to you.

PSALM 86:5

Long ago a well-publicized experiment proved that humans need love. In an orphanage in the Soviet Union half of the infants received kisses and hugs from their caretakers, while the other half received only feeding and changing. In a short time, the unloved infants began to weaken, while their cuddled counterparts thrived.

God created us with this need to be loved, yet only he offers an unconditional love that can fill our souls and minister to our deepest need.

S.M.H.

AS YOU PRAY TODAY:

- Recognize your need for God's love. Accept his love and let it fill you to overflowing.
- Rejoice in the knowledge that God loves you unconditionally. You don't have to do or be anything special to get it.
- Ask God to show you how you can share his love with others.

DISTRIBUTION AND PRODUCTION

God . . . reconciled us to himself through Christ and gave us the ministry of reconciliation.

2 Corinthians 5:18

Our *prayers* of intercession are an extension of his *work* of intercession. The difference is in distributing versus producing. We don't have to produce anything—reconciliation, deliverance, victory, etc.—but rather we distribute, as the disciples did with the loaves and fishes. We don't deliver anyone; we don't reconcile anyone to God. The work is already done. Reconciliation is complete. Salvation is complete. Finished! And yet . . . we [are used by God through our prayers] for the release and application of these things.

Dutch Sheets

AS YOU PRAY TODAY:

- Remember that Christ is the ultimate, final and only mediator between you and God the Father.
- Pray "in Jesus' name," asking him to intercede for you.
- Intercede for others. In doing so you are representing Christ and what he has already accomplished.

HELTER SKELTER CHOICES

Your ears will hear a voice behind you, saying, "This is the way; walk in it."

ISAIAH 30:21

Sometimes we watch as our friends or family ask the Lord to guide their decisions, but then they head off in the direction they think they ought to go without waiting for God's answer. We do the same thing ourselves sometimes. Experience proves that this kind of impatience is rarely productive.

Yet God says, "Be still." If we give God a chance, he will give us the wisdom to follow the direction he has chosen for us. That's the key to every decision our friends, family, and we, will ever make—patiently waiting for God's answer, rather than making helter-skelter choices that they may only regret later on.

S.M.H.

AS YOU PRAY TODAY:

- Pray that God will remind your friends of his sovereignty.
- Intercede for their patience to await God's answer when they seek his direction.
- Ask that God will fill them with strength to follow his will.

A HELPING HAND

Love your neighbor as yourself. I am the LORD.

LEVITICUS 19:18

Across the vast continent of Asia a rumor circulates: if you need help in America, find a building with a cross; these people will help you. Hundreds of students coming to America to study from foreign lands find that rumor true in the helping hands of para-church ministries. One organization locates near large university campuses and helps international students find housing, furniture, and furnishings. They offer Bible study classes, too, as a means of helping foreign students perfect their English language skills. In the process these students hear the Gospel—some for the very first time.

S.M.H.

AS YOU PRAY TODAY:

- Lift to God the para-church ministries who reach out to foreign students—they need staffing, support, and creativity.
- Pray for the students who come to these American missionaries for help—they need open hearts to hear the Gospel.

ZONED OUT

Fight for your brothers, your sons and your daughters, your wives and your homes.

NEHEMIAH 4:14

The Purple Passion opened next door to Union High School today. There were no grand opening signs. The owner didn't want to call attention to this adult bookstore for fear of reprisals. He needn't have worried. No one had shown up for the zoning commission meetings or even filed a written complaint about this seeming violation of the decency laws. People were too zoned out to tune in to the changes in their neighborhood.

In an interview following the meeting, a zoning commissioner stated, "If *anyone* had complained, we could have stopped this. But the only person in today's meeting was the shopkeeper. So ... what could we do?"

S.M.H.

AS YOU PRAY TODAY:

- Find out the names your zoning commissioners. Pray for each one.
- Pray for the meetings and decisions.
- Ask God to open your eyes to ways that you can stop evil and indecency from invading your neighborhood.

CHECHNYA'S ETERNAL DESTINY

[Salvation] is the gift of God—not by works, so that no one can boast.

EPHESIANS 2:8–9

The republic of Chechnya is nestled along the northern slopes of the Caucasus Mountains. Plagued by hostilities with Russia since it began fighting for its independence, Chechnya has seen many of its people killed or displaced. The majority of Chechens are Sunni Muslims who believe they can win eternal life by accumulating enough good deeds to offset their bad ones. Righteous men are guaranteed a place in Paradise, but women have few rights and are fearful of what awaits them after death.

AS YOU PRAY TODAY:

- Ask God to open Chechen eyes to the free gift of salvation.
- Pray that Chechen children will have the opportunity to hear the Gospel and be sure of their eternal destiny.
- Intercede for willing workers to bring God's love to Chechnya.

CONSTANT FORGIVENESS

If we confess our sins, God is faithful and just and will forgive us our sins.

1 JOHN 1:9

When we confess our failings to God, he willingly offers us forgiveness. We can count on it. He will not refuse to forgive even if we make another mistake. Yet there may be times when we don't *feel* forgiven, times when we feel we've crossed an invisible line, and God will give up on us. The Bible reassures us that though our feelings are fleeting, God's forgiveness is constant. If we confess our sins, he *will* forgive us. It's a promise we can bank on. And it's a promise we can share with others, too.

S.M.H.

AS YOU PRAY TODAY:

- Seek God's mercy for your sins. Pray for illumination as you search your heart.
- Receive God's cleansing deep within. Let him wash your soul and fill you with his holiness.
- Claim his protection against the temptation to doubt his forgiveness.

MICAIAH'S METTLE

Micaiah said, "As surely as the LORD lives, I can tell him only what my God says."

2 CHRONICLES 18:13

Oh, to have the courage and mettle of Micaiah! To stand before kings and naysayers and speak God's truth. How many times do we capitulate and speak sugar-coated, soothing words to those around us because we want to be liked or accepted? Though there are times for soothing, comforting words, there are other times when we need to speak out against an injustice even if it means we will be rebuffed or rejected. Micaiah knew when and what to speak because he measured his words against a godly yardstick. Do we?

S.M.H.

AS YOU PRAY TODAY:

- Ask God to give you discernment to know when to speak and when to be silent.
- Pray for the courage of Micaiah to speak up boldly when you see injustice or ungodly behavior.
- Resolve to measure all of your words by Micaiah's godly yardstick.

A BLESSED UNION

Honor one another above yourselves.

ROMANS 12:10

One of the great challenges of marriage is learning to live with another person. All too often we treat strangers with more kindness than we do our own spouse. Yet, if we took time to remember the days before our marriage, we might catch a glimpse of the excitement, anticipation, and joy that we felt toward our intended mate. When we married our spouse, we chose to love each other for a lifetime. We need to renew that choice daily. We need to look for God's Spirit in each other and respond to that Spirit in love. And we need to honor and bless each other every day—in words and actions.

S.M.H.

AS YOU PRAY TODAY:

- Find time to pray together and thank God for your spouse.
- Pray for the needs on each heart.
- Ask God to bless your marriage with abundant love and forgiveness.
- If you're not married, pray a blessing over the marriage of someone in your family or circle of friends.

VIGILANT EDUCATION

"I will instruct you and teach you in the way you should go," says the Lord.

PSALM 32:8

Christian primary and secondary schools have existed for decades. But Christian colleges and universities actually trace their lineage to the founding of our country. Some of our most prestigious universities began as Bible schools and seminaries.

Yet worldly influences and secular philosophies have wreaked havoc on these institutions of higher learning. Many Christian colleges have had to water down their standards and remove courses from their curriculum because of pressure from civil rights groups.

Our Christian colleges and universities need our vigilance, our financial support, and our prayers. If we don't support these institutions, we may lose them.

S.M.H.

AS YOU PRAY TODAY:

- Thank God for colleges that adhere to strong, Christian principles.
- Pray for God's blessing on the deans and professors of these schools.
- Ask God to send students who are committed to higher education and Christian ethics.

KEEP IT CLEAN

There is a time for everything . . . a time to keep and a time to throw away.

ECCLESIASTES 3:1, 6

Television news photos showed piles of garbage lining New York City's streets during a recent sanitation workers' strike. Heat and humidity turned the piles into fetid heaps that assaulted people's senses whenever they left a building's confines. When the strike was finally settled, workers toiled for days to remove the mountains of rubbish.

Some of us live in rural areas and are responsible for our own garbage disposal. Yet urban dwellers depend on sanitation workers to keep neighborhoods clean. Without their dedicated service, rats and disease would run rampant in our cities. Let's find time to say, "Thank you!"

S.M.H.

AS YOU PRAY TODAY:

- Count sanitation workers among God's blessings today.
- Pray for safety as they ride on the backs of trucks and place themselves in traffic lanes.
- Ask God for an opportunity to say thanks to your sanitation workers.

THE SPIRITS OF ZIMBABWE

Those troubled by evil spirits were cured.

LUKE 6:18

Zimbabwe boasts spectacular scenery, thunderous waterfalls, and one of the world's largest man-made lakes. Yet racial tensions run high in Zimbabwe, and many people are hungry or unemployed, especially the thousands of refugees from neighboring warring nations. Though Christianity is allowed in Zimbabwe, many people still live under the control of tribal chiefs, who are chosen by spirit rituals. Zimbabweans need to be set free from the power of evil spirits.

AS YOU PRAY TODAY:

- Ask God to give Zimbabwean Christians the strength to stand firm against spirit worship.
- Pray for a lessening of racial tension so that Zimbabweans of different tribes and colors can live together in harmony.
- Intercede for missionaries and native workers who minister to the poor, the unemployed, and refugees.

THE KING'S MANIFESTO

The LORD Almighty has sworn, "Surely, as I have planned, so it will be, and as I have purposed, so it will stand."

ISAIAH 14:24

In the Persian Empire a king's decree, once sealed with his signet ring, was unchangeable. Yet God's words to us are more powerful than any earthly king's manifesto. With a word from God, authorities are established and other kingdoms toppled. God's Word formed everything in creation, and his Word declares the gift of salvation to those who believe in Jesus Christ. God's words promise us an eternity in heaven and a strength to carry us through the problems of this life. God's words are powerful, life-changing, and irrevocable. Consider his words to you; and be thankful.

S.M.H.

AS YOU PRAY TODAY:

- Reflect on God's promises to be your comfort, healer, strength, guide, and peace.
- Claim God's promises of provision, protection, and presence.
- Rejoice in his words of forgiveness, assurance, mercy, and grace.

ALONE IN THE WILDERNESS

Wait for the LORD;
be strong and take heart
and wait for the LORD.

PSALM 27:14

God, where are you? Are you playing cat and mouse with me, or are your purposes larger than my perceptions? I feel alone, lost, forsaken.

You showed yourself to Abraham, Isaac, and Jacob. When Moses wanted to know what you looked like, you obliged him. Why them and not me?

I am tired of praying . . . of asking . . . of waiting. But I will keep on praying and asking and waiting because I have nowhere else to go. I do not understand. But I know that you are out to do me good.

RICHARD FOSTER

AS YOU PRAY TODAY:

- As you face your own wilderness, make this prayer your own.
- Remember that trust comes before faith; so trust and wait for God to do you good.
- Realize that the wilderness is never permanent; there will come a time of revelation and rest.

CHILDREN OF INTEGRITY

You desire truth in the inner parts
you teach me wisdom in the inmost place, O Lord.

PSALM 51:6

All parents want to think that their children are honest. When we discover that one of our kids has deceived us, we are devastated. Lord, help my children to feel your delight when they speak the truth and to remember that you hate it when we lie (Proverbs 12:22). When they persevere toward truth, may they feel great freedom of spirit (John 8:32)—so much so that the passing reward of a lie looks as cheap and fleeting as it really is. Amen.

DAVID & HEATHER KOPP

AS YOU PRAY TODAY:

- Pray that your children will learn that God desires truth in their hearts (Psalm 51:6).
- Pray God's protection on your children because wickedness is present everywhere (Psalm 12:2).
- Ask God to encourage honesty in the small things your children handle now, knowing that one day they will be entrusted with much more (Matthew 25:21).

THE ENDS OF THE EARTH

"Bring my salvation to the ends of the earth,"
says the Lord.

ISAIAH 49:6

A sign above the exit doors in a church proclaims, "You are now entering your mission field." While many parishioners share the Gospel with their local family, friends, and co-workers, others travel to foreign lands with the good news of Christ. These missionaries face the daily challenges of life while enduring the difficulties of living in a foreign culture. They are God's messengers abroad who need our personal support and intercession on a daily basis.

S.M.H.

AS YOU PRAY TODAY:

- Pray for a foreign missionary family that your church supports. Learn their names, where they are assigned, and what they are doing.
- Pray for the specific needs mentioned in their prayer letters.
- Foreign missionaries are just like you. Whatever may be troubling you today may be troubling a missionary, too. Ask God to resolve that problem for both of you.

LOVE YOUR NEIGHBOR

Love your neighbor as yourself.

MATTHEW 19:19

How many times do we sit before God and give him our list of needs and wants? Probably too often. For once though, our seemingly selfish ways can be helpful. Since Jesus told us to love our neighbors like we love ourselves, one tangible way of doing this is to *pray* for our neighbors in the same way that we pray for ourselves. We can talk to our neighbors and ask them if they have specific needs we could pray for. And as we bring our own requests to God for provision, protection, or personal needs, we can ask him to provide the same blessings for our neighbors.

MIKE WILSON

AS YOU PRAY TODAY:

- Ask for the Lord's blessing on your neighbors.
- Pray that God will reveal himself to your neighbors in a new and exciting way.
- Intercede for a specific need that you see in your neighbor's life.

LISTENING TO THE LIGHT

You were once darkness, but now you are light in the Lord. Live as children of light.

EPHESIANS 5:8

In the late 1960s a radio station in Hinche began broadcasting the salvation message to Haiti. For many years this ministry reached people all over the Central Plateau, but an embargo on U.S. imports ultimately silenced Radio Lumière and its Gospel message.

Recently a crew from World Gospel Mission returned to Hinche, repaired the antenna, installed a solar-powered electrical system, and readied the studio and its equipment to broadcast local programming. Once again the people of Haiti can listen to the light of God's good news in their own language.

DALE DOROTHY

AS YOU PRAY TODAY:

- Ask God to provide the funds, materials, and personnel needed for Radio Lumière.
- Pray that God will open new opportunities in film and television.
- Intercede for the people of Haiti, long-bound by voodoo and superstition, to turn to Christ.

THE ALL-KNOWING GOD

The LORD says ... I know what is going through your mind.

EZEKIEL 11:5

God does not merely note your actions; he does not simply notice what the appearance of your countenance is. God sees what you are thinking of; he looks within. He does not want you to tell him what you are thinking about—he can see that. He can read right through you. He knows every thought, every imagination, every conception. He even knows unformed imagination—the thought scarcely shot from the bow, reserved in the quiver of the mind. He sees it all, every particle, every atom of it.

CHARLES H. SPURGEON

AS YOU PRAY TODAY:

- Ask God to purify your desires and needs and satisfy them with himself.
- Fix your purposes on God's will, not on the distractions of wealth, ease, and others' opinions.
- Resolve to walk uprightly, and bring every thought captive to God's control.

STEALING BY DEGREES

The serpent ... said to the woman, "Did God really say 'You must not eat from any tree in the garden'?"

GENESIS 3:1

As the husbandman digs about the root of a tree, by degrees loosens it, and at last it falls, Satan steals by degrees into the heart. He did not say to Eve at first, "Eat the apple." No, but he goes more subtly to work. He puts forth a question, "Hath God said?" Surely, Eve, thou art mistaken; the bountiful God never intended to debar thee one of the best trees of the garden. "Hath God said?" By degrees he wrought her to distrust. Then she took of the fruit and ate.

THOMAS WATSON

AS YOU PRAY TODAY:

- Ask God to make you aware of Satan's first attempts to tempt you.
- Pray that God will help you oppose the beginnings of evil.
- Commit to strengthen your heart in Christ by daily Bible study and prayer.

ROLE MODELS

Train a child in the way he should go,
and when he is old he will not turn from it.

PROVERBS 22:6

It is an awesome responsibility to teach children. And it is our responsibility to know our children's teachers and to know what they are being taught. Youth ministers, Sunday School teachers, tutors, school teachers, and coaches all play a role in our children's upbringing. While parents are the primary role models for their children, our children's teachers will mold them, too. We must choose carefully these people who will become our substitute role models, for we will have to live with their influence for years to come.

S.M.H.

AS YOU PRAY TODAY:

- Pray for the strength to continue to be a good role model for your children.
- Ask God to provide teachers who are good examples for your children.
- Rejoice in the good Christian leadership that your children have already.

CONSIDER THE HOMELESS

Jesus said, "Whatever you did for one of the least of these brothers of mine, you did for me."

MATTHEW 25:40

It's easy for us to forget what we don't see everyday. It's easy to neglect what we aren't reminded to remember. It's easy for us to ignore so much. But God wants us to consider and care for those less fortunate than ourselves. Many of our communities provide shelters for the homeless, but these shelters always need of food, clothing, and volunteers. God wants us to consider the homeless—not just at Thanksgiving and Christmas time—but every day of the year.

CONOVER SWOFFORD

AS YOU PRAY TODAY:

- Pray for those in your community who have no homes. Ask God to give them a safe place to live.
- Pray for funding and staffing for shelters and soup kitchens that minister to the homeless.
- Pray for an opportunity to show God's love through volunteering at a homeless shelter.

STATE HOUSE STATUTES

The LORD gives wisdom,
and from his mouth come knowledge
and understanding.

PROVERBS 2:6

Some of us avoid politics—discussions of it, involvement in it—because we find it unsettling. Daniel took a different view. In the government of the Medes and Persians, any law signed by the king could not be repealed. Daniel stood among Persian leaders who made recommendations to the king about which laws to enact. And without the mediating effect of Daniel's witness, one day ungodly legislation met the king's seal, and Daniel met a lion's den.

S.M.H.

AS YOU PRAY TODAY:

- Pray that God gives your legislators the ability to see the implications of their decisions.
- Recall the policies pending in your state house. Pray that God will have mercy and bring about only those things that will be beneficial.
- Ask God's blessing on your legislators. They need wisdom, integrity, and godly values.

A POLITICAL TIME BOMB

Blessed are you when men hate you . . .
because of the Son of Man.

LUKE 6:22

After a bitter war of liberation, Algeria declared independence from France in 1962. Though a one party socialist regime has held onto power for many years, Algeria has become a political time bomb due to economic failures and political abuses. Government leaders have actively encouraged the development of an Islamic-Arab socialist state, prohibiting the proclamation of the Gospel. In recent years, Algerian Christians have suffered increasingly intense persecution from members of Muslim extremist groups, and believers must meet in secret because of intimidation from family and friends.

AS YOU PRAY TODAY:

- Pray for the relaxing of opposition to the Gospel in Algeria.
- Ask God to overrule in the government to bring religious freedom and political moderation to Algeria.
- Intercede for boldness for Algerian Christians to share their faith and bring others to Christ despite persecution and intimidation.

APPROACHABLE HOLINESS

Let us ... approach the throne of grace with confidence, so that we may receive mercy and find grace to help us in our time of need.

HEBREWS 4:16

Most of us probably will never be invited to the White House to sit down and talk with the president. Most of us can't walk through the door of a state representative without an appointment made months in advance. And most of us wouldn't even be able to drop in unannounced on our pastor and find him in his office, available for a chat. Yet God, the Creator of the universe, says that we can come before him at any time, for any reason, and he will not turn us away. He is holy; and he is approachable.

S.M.H.

AS YOU PRAY TODAY:

- Thank God for the accessibility he has granted us to come before him in our prayers.
- Humbly ask forgiveness for not honoring God as you should.
- Rejoice that God cares about your plans, your concerns, and your life.

WHY OR WHY NOT?

In God, whose word I praise,
in the LORD, whose word I praise—
in God I trust; I will not be afraid.
What can man do to me?

PSALM 56:10–11

The Israelites had been miraculously delivered from slavery. They had walked on dry ground through the Red Sea. Yet, a few weeks later, they were discouraged and hungry. Difficulties obscured the promised land, so the Israelites cried, "Why?" and talked about returning to Egypt. Often when we face discouragement we echo their doubter's cry. Though we might want to "go back" to our comfort zones, we should put the discouraging question "Why?" aside and ask instead "Why not?" We serve an Almighty God who is able to bring about his plans. *Why not* trust him to fulfill them?

S.M.H.

AS YOU PRAY TODAY:

- Confess your certainty in God's sovereignty despite outward circumstances.
- Center your thoughts on God's plan for your life.
- Trust God's promise to always be with you and lead you safely home.

MONEY, MONEY, MONEY

Do not worry, saying, "What shall we eat?" or "What shall we drink?" ... But seek first God's kingdom and his righteousness, and all these things will be given to you as well.

MATTHEW 6:31, 33

How often we fret about financial problems. Our worries increase if we have extended family. We act as if worrying shows that we are truly concerned about our financial difficulties. And we seem to think God can handle everything but our money.

Our friends often follow this warped reasoning, too. Yet the Bible urges us to be good stewards of God's gifts and trust God for everything, including our money. Just as little children trust their parents to provide for them, we and our friends should trust our heavenly Father to care for our needs, too.

S.M.H.

AS YOU PRAY TODAY:

- Turn your friends' financial needs and worries over to God.
- Ask God to help you bless your friends during their financial struggles.
- Thank God for his blessings, care, and provision for your friends.

MINISTERING TO THE FORGOTTEN

I was in prison and you came to visit me.

MATTHEW 25:36

Years ago a young man broke the law and was sent to prison. He was bitter and resentful, but members of his church prayed for him and visited him. Two years into his sentence, his resentfulness melted, and the young man put his trust in Jesus. He became God's ambassador in prison and obtained permission to start a Bible study for his fellow inmates. A young man's life was changed because a church group cared enough to minister to someone who could have easily been forgotten.

CONOVER SWOFFORD

AS YOU PRAY TODAY:

- Remember those who minister faithfully in prisons—chaplains and laypeople.
- Ask God to raise up volunteers to work with inmates to teach them skills they can use on the outside.
- Pray that God will move in the hearts of inmates and cause them to come to him in faith.

CITY GOVERNMENT

The authorities are God's servants,
who give their full time to governing.

ROMANS 13:6

Can you name your city council members? Do you know your township supervisor or city manager? These people oversee the smooth running of municipal departments and decide issues of public interest from making sure sidewalks are accessible for the handicapped to ensuring that city employees get paid on time. Yet these civil servants face the same problems we do. If someone in their family is ill, their attention can be divided between family and civic responsibilities. We should treat them as we would want to be treated, and that includes praying for them often.

S.M.H.

AS YOU PRAY TODAY:

- Bring each member of your city council to God. Request God's wisdom for each one.
- Intercede for city council or township meetings that God will guide the discussions and decisions.
- Ask God's blessing on your city or township leaders—both in their personal and public lives.

A MIXED MESSAGE

Do not follow other gods, the gods of the peoples around you; for the L*ORD your God, who is among you, is a jealous God.*

DEUTERONOMY 6:14–15

Western Samoa is a beautiful, island nation in the South Pacific. Each day at dusk bells ring, summoning Samoans to a time of prayer, singing, and Bible reading. Most Samoans claim to be Christians, worshiping several times a week and often attending early morning prayer meetings. But sadly, many Samoans have mixed the message of the Gospel with Mormonism and ancient customs that honor evil spirits. Christianity is merely a part of their culture, rather than a meaningful relationship with a Savior.

AS YOU PRAY TODAY:

- Ask God to help godly Samoan Christians speak out against the mixed messages of faith that are readily accepted.
- Pray that church leaders in Western Samoa will give God's Word its rightful place in worship.
- Pray that the growth of Mormonism will be checked.

IN EVERY PLACE

The LORD God Almighty will be with you.

AMOS 5:14

What inferences should we draw from the fact that God is in every place? If you believe that God is about your bed and about your path and spies out all your ways, then take care not to do the least thing, speak the least word, indulge the least thought that you think would offend him. Approve your ways to his all-seeing eyes, so that he may say to your hearts what he will proclaim aloud in the great assembly of men and angels, "Well done, good and faithful servant!" (Matthew 25:21).

JOHN WESLEY

AS YOU PRAY TODAY:

- Cheerfully expect that the always-present God will guide you in all your ways.
- Trust that he will hold you in the hollow of his hand.
- Claim his promise to establish, strengthen, and settle you in your faith.

HEIRS TO THE KINGDOM

We are heirs—heirs of God and co-heirs with Christ.

ROMANS 8:17

Parents face an uphill battle when urging children to do and be their best. Too often children prefer to take the easy way with life. But good parents recognize that they have to help their children set goals and achieve them.

Our heavenly Father helps us, his "spiritual" children, grow and learn, too. Some days we willingly follow his direction, but other days we wander off on our own. Yet God doesn't give up on us. We are heirs to his kingdom. He wants us to move beyond where we are to become more like him.

S.M.H.

AS YOU PRAY TODAY:

- Ask God to show you his goals for your life.
- Trust him even when his ways and purposes seem unclear.
- Rejoice in your status as God's child, recognizing all of the rights and responsibilities befitting an heir to his kingdom.

BLESS 'EM GOOD!

When a period of feasting had run its course, Job would send and have [his children] purified. Early in the morning Job would sacrifice a burnt offering for each of them.

JOB 1:5

Can you picture Job? After his kids spent the night partying, Job rises at the crack of dawn to offer a sacrifice for each of his ten children. Can you see him standing there? The kids are probably still in bed; the servants are getting breakfast ready. And here's Job, standing beside the altar, saying something like, "I don't know if my kids have said or done anything to offend you, Lord. They're good kids, Lord. Forgive 'em, and bless 'em good!" Job cared enough about his kids to pray God's forgiveness and blessing on them. What an example for us to follow!

S.M.H.

AS YOU PRAY TODAY:

- Tell God about your children. Name them each by name.
- Ask that your children repent—for sins of ignorance and sins "on purpose."
- Pray God's blessing on your children—every day!

RADIO WAVES

Faith comes from hearing the message, and the message is heard through the word of Christ.

ROMANS 10:17

Radio waves can reach places no person can. Christian radio broadcasts stream into countries closed to traditional missionary efforts because of location or governmental restrictions. In HCJB (Heralding Christ Jesus Blessing) World Radio's offices in Quito, Ecuador, a lighted signboard indicates places that have been reached with its Gospel broadcasts. Letters from listeners—some smuggled out of countries hostile to the Gospel—are tacked on a bulletin board nearby, reminding all who visit that God's Word is life changing.

S.M.H.

AS YOU PRAY TODAY:

- Remember the ministry of HCJB and radio stations like it that send the Gospel message around the world.
- Ask God to provide the personnel, equipment, and support needed to keep these stations on the air.
- Claim God's promise that his words will reach responsive hearts.

FAMILY SERVICES

How good and pleasant it is when brothers live together in unity!

PSALM 133:1

In our society, the "system" has a bad reputation. The news media has seized on some stories of foster care abuse, family court atrocities, or a social worker's mistreatment of a child, giving all members of the family protective services a bad name. In reality the majority of these people work hard to make Psalm 133 a reality in the lives of struggling families, to make each home a better, safer place for children, and to teach families how to live together in unity.

S.M.H.

AS YOU PRAY TODAY:

- Pray for our country, that families would turn and seek God's will and way in their lives.
- Ask God to show you how you could reach out to a struggling family in your community.
- Pray that God will give family protective services personnel the moral and emotional strength needed to carry out their jobs day after day.

MONGOLIAN JUSTICE?

Peter was kept in prison, but the church was earnestly praying to God for him.

ACTS 12:5

A young Mongolian medical doctor reportedly came to know Christ through radio broadcasts in his native Kazakh language. The young doctor was arrested last summer and sentenced to thirteen years in a prison labor camp in western Mongolia. Police officials charged him with "distributing the wrong religious propaganda" and telling others about Christ. Only the Buddhist and Islamic faiths may be legally shared in Mongolia.

AS YOU PRAY TODAY:

- Earnestly pray for imprisoned Christians in Mongolia and an early release from prison.
- Pray that God will give them strength to withstand the torture and harassment given to Christian prisoners.
- Continue to pray for other believers in Mongolia and for the work of radio broadcasts to reach other souls for Christ.

UNITED OPPOSITES

"I will lay waste the mountains and hills and . . . I will turn the darkness into light before them," says the Lord.

ISAIAH 42:15–16

All the terribleness of God is the good man's security. When the good man sees God wasting the mountains and the hills, he does not say, "I must worship him or he will destroy me." He says, "The beneficent side of that power is all mine." Power has become to him an assurance of rest. He says, "My Father has infinite resources of judgment, and every one of them is to my trusting heart a signal of unsearchable riches of mercy."

JOSEPH PARKER

AS YOU PRAY TODAY:

- Consider the seeming opposites of God's nature: love and judgment, destroyer and friend.
- Do not give in to fear like, "Be good, or God will crush you." That message is sin, not liberty.
- Rejoice that God's mighty power is an assurance of rest, love, and his mercy for you.

EXPRESSING GRATITUDE

Give thanks in all circumstances, for this is God's will for you in Christ Jesus.

1 THESSALONIANS 5:18

One summer I took my son Todd to the county fair. We enjoyed some rides, and my tired little boy fell asleep in the back seat as we started home. A few minutes down the highway, though, he had his arms around my shoulders. "Dad, I want to thank you for taking me to that fair," he said. His words moved me so much, I felt like turning the car around and going back for round two! God is our Father, and he, too, is moved when we express our thanksgiving.

BILL HYBELS

AS YOU PRAY TODAY:

- Thank God for the obvious answers to prayer that you have received.
- Praise him for the material blessings that he has given you.
- Rejoice in the relationship you share together and the spiritual blessings he provides.

BREAK BAD HABITS

May God arise, may his enemies be scattered.

PSALM 68:1

We are soldiers of the light. He has given us his light; he has given us his sword; he has given us his name. Allow him to shine through you. Wield the laser sword of the Spirit. How destructive to darkness is his lightning sword. Station yourself spiritually in front of your rebellious children and ask God to send a bolt of meekness to them. Aim the light of liberty at their addictions, whether drugs, sex, alcohol, or whatever. Ask God to shine forth, breaking through the darkness of deception. As the Israelites carried the presence and glory of God into battle, so must we.

DUTCH SHEETS

AS YOU PRAY TODAY:

- Boldly ask God to release his power in your family.
- Ask God to break the bad habits that control your family.
- Claim God's promises of wholeness, strength, and freedom for your family.

DOOR TO DOOR

Jesus said, "You will receive power when the Holy Spirit comes on you; and you will be my witnesses in Jerusalem, and in all Judea and Samaria, and to the ends of the earth."

ACTS 1:8

Jesus told his disciples to begin sharing the Gospel where they were—in Jerusalem. The disciples first brought the good news of Christ to people they knew, to family, friends, and neighbors. Paul's missionary journeys, too, started close to home and moved outward to other cities. Our witness, like theirs, should begin where we live. We can begin door-to-door evangelism with the people we know in our neighborhood—the folks next door on our right and the people next door on our left.

CONOVER SWOFFORD

AS YOU PRAY TODAY:

- Rejoice that God has given you a wonderful message to share with others.
- Pray that he will open a way for you to share the Gospel with one of your neighbors this week.
- Ask God to give you the right words to say and to prepare hearts to hear his words.

A CIVIC PRIVILEGE

This is what the LORD Almighty says: "Administer true justice; show mercy and compassion to one another."

ZECHARIAH 7:9

A friend remarked that she wasn't a registered voter. When asked why not, she responded that she didn't want to register because then she could be chosen for jury duty. And jury duty would be inconvenient and take too long and be tough to decide. Her list of excuses went on and on. Yet a call to serve on a jury is a civic privilege, a new opportunity to learn about our justice system, a chance to let God's wisdom shine in a dark place. This list goes on and on, too!

S.M.H.

AS YOU PRAY TODAY:

- Pray for the jury selection process and your own response to being called as a juror.
- Thank God for the freedoms that are safeguarded by our justice system.
- Pray that jurors who serve will be honest and careful listeners, able to put prejudice aside and to correctly judge the truth.

THE LAND OF SHEBA

When the queen of Sheba heard about the fame of Solomon and his relation to the name of the LORD, she came to test him with hard questions.

1 KINGS 10:1

The Queen of Sheba's kingdom lies buried under the Arabian desert in Yemen. In 1990 the two lands of North Yemen and South Yemen united, but conflict over religious issues has provoked tensions that threaten to destroy this country's uneasy peace. Witnessing for Christ is limited by governmental restrictions and the prevailing Muslim belief that Christianity is only for slaves. Many Yemenis also believe that all people from Western nations are Christians. The poor behavior of some soldiers and tourists has cast a cloud on any Christian witness.

AS YOU PRAY TODAY:

- Intercede for Yemenis to see God's wisdom as the Queen of Sheba did.
- Pray that godly believers will come from the West to fill open positions in hospitals and schools.
- Ask God to strengthen and encourage the small Christian element in Yemen, making their faith a light to darkened souls.

THE GOD WHO SEES

You are the God who sees me.

GENESIS 16:13

God sees you as much as if there were nobody else in the world for him to look at. The infinite mind of God is able to grasp a million objects at once and yet to focus as much on one as if there were nothing else but that one . . . as much, as entirely, as absolutely without division of sight, as if you were the only being his hands had ever made. Can you grasp that? God sees you with the whole of his sight—you! You are the particular object of his attention at this very moment.

CHARLES H. SPURGEON

AS YOU PRAY TODAY:

- Contemplate the thought that God sees you entirely, constantly, completely.
- Know that because he sees you, he also knows your every need even before you speak it.
- Pray to see as God sees, to focus on the things that are important to him.

REST FROM STRESS

Jesus said, "Come with me by yourselves to a quiet place and get some rest."

MARK 6:31

Beginning swimmers kick and paddle with ferocity, but rarely do they cover much distance before they become exhausted. A good swimmer knows that a swimming stroke must allow the body a brief rest time. No matter how efficient a swimmer's arms and legs may be, unless there is a regular time in each stroke when the arms and legs can rest, the swimmer will tire. In the same way, we need to find time to rest if we, too, want to maintain efficiency.

S.M.H.

AS YOU PRAY TODAY:

- Bring your busy schedule to God and ask him to prioritize it.
- Hear Jesus' admonition to "get some rest" and sit quietly in his presence.
- Resolve to withhold adding commitments to an overcrowded schedule, knowing exhaustion and efficiency do not walk hand-in-hand.

TENDER LOVING CARE

We can comfort those in any trouble with the comfort we ourselves have received from God.

2 CORINTHIANS 1:4

Rough times define us, change us, and illumine for us those who are our true friends. We all have friends and family who stick by us no matter what happens. God cares for us, too, by lovingly sending us someone to lean on. We are blessed with people we can turn to in our struggles who will welcome us and our problems. And later on we can return God's loving care by helping someone else who needs support. God's comfort flows *to* us when needed and *through* us when others need it.

S.M.H.

AS YOU PRAY TODAY:

- Thank God for the loving support of your family and friends.
- Receive the comfort God offers you through them.
- Ask him to show you ways that you can share his tender, loving care to others.

THE WINGS OF A DOVE

"Even while you sleep among the campfires, the wings of my dove are sheathed with silver, its feathers with shining gold," says the Lord.

PSALM 68:13

It looked like a big, white dove. But this bird wasn't a dove. It was a single engine Cessna bringing needed supplies to missionaries deep in the Amazon jungle.

For many years missionary aviation has filled a need for Christian mission organizations, Bible translators, and indigenous people. A short flight can save a missionary days or weeks of strenuous travel on rough roads, mountain paths, or jungle rivers. Providing this transportation is the calling and mission of organizations like JAARS and Missionary Aviation Fellowship—God's wings of love.

S.M.H.

AS YOU PRAY TODAY:

- Ask God to raise up qualified pilots and mechanics to keep these planes flying.
- Pray for support personnel as they record logs and account information.
- Intercede for health, safety, and accurate weather reports—all of which affect flights.

IT'S A TRAGEDY

Blessed are the merciful, for they will be shown mercy.

MATTHEW 5:7

Severe weather is a normal occurrence in many parts of our country. Northern climates suffer blizzards, ice storms, and deadly temperatures. Other areas are affected with tornadoes, hurricanes, or floods. When severe weather passes, it leaves destruction in its wake. That's when towns and neighbors show their true colors. Banding together each one helps the other, regardless of church affiliation or other distinctions. Reaching out, giving, sharing, working together—blessing each other as God has blessed them.

CONOVER SWOFFORD

AS YOU PRAY TODAY:

- Pray for the victims of tragedies—weather-related, natural disasters, or criminal activity.
- Intercede for aid agencies that work with tragedy victims that they will be understanding, efficient, and fair.
- Ask God to show you how you can help when tragedies affect your community. Do you need to learn CPR, serve on a disaster committee, or volunteer with the Red Cross?

JUCHE

The eyes of the blind be opened and the ears of the deaf unstopped.

ISAIAH 35:5

North Korea is an isolated nation, closed to the rest of the world. Christians, who must worship in secret, are often hunted down and killed. In the late 1960s, Kim Il Sung introduced a cultic belief system that blended Christianity with Communist terminology and self-reliance. Known as Juche, this ideology took firm root in North Korea and permeates every aspect of the culture. Through the use of rigid religious controls, the people are forced to worship their dictator as an omniscient, omnipresent god who supposedly can part the clouds and cause trees to blossom.

THOMAS J. BELKE AND STEVE CLEARY

AS YOU PRAY TODAY:

- Pray fervently for God to open the blinded minds of Juche adherents.
- Ask God to strengthen and protect believers in North Korea.
- Intercede for an open economy so that North Korea can receive needed supplies and an open route to sharing the Gospel.

THE MIGHTY ONE

The Mighty One, God, the LORD!

JOSHUA 22:22

The Israelites were suspicious of the tribes of Reuben, Gad and the half-tribe of Manasseh because of an altar they had set up at Geliloth (Joshua 22:10). It looked like these tribes intended to desert God, and the Israelites were ready to go to war. This brief confession of faith assured everyone that all the tribes were united under the "the Mighty One." Their words of reverence toward God removed the threat of war and reunited a nation.

S.M.H.

AS YOU PRAY TODAY:

- Review the ways you speak about God. Are your words full of reverence?
- Review your actions—as you drive, work, interact with others. Do your actions reflect a reverence for God?
- Review what it means to serve the "Mighty One, God, the Lord!" Do you live like you believe these words?

COMPLETE HONESTY

May integrity and uprightness protect me,
because my hope is in you, O Lord.

Psalm 25:21

Maggie had been caught with a stolen piece of candy. Her mother insisted that she return to the market and tell the shopkeeper what she had done. After hearing her confession, the shopkeeper gave her a stern warning about thievery. But when Maggie told her father, his look of disappointment was harder to bear than any punishment exacted by the shopkeeper. Maggie wept, knowing that a penny candy had separated her from her father's loving smile. And Maggie vowed that she would never displease her father in such a way again.

S.M.H.

AS YOU PRAY TODAY:

- Ask your heavenly Father to help you make your words truthful and honest.
- Pray that your actions will be full of integrity.

HIGHLY REGARDED

In your hands are strength and power to exalt and give strength to all, O Lord.

1 CHRONICLES 29:12

If you're concerned that your loved ones find meaning in their jobs and high regard for their work, make this your prayer today:

Father, thank you for giving my loved ones wisdom in every decision they must make at work today. Help them to give their employers a full day's work for a full day's pay.

Show my loved ones their mistakes so that they can correct them, and give them understanding on how to be more effective and efficient with their time. May their enthusiasm for their work be evident to others. And, no matter what the situation, let them respond as you would, letting their light shine with your love and truth.

Grant my loved ones the knowledge that you will exalt them and give them strength to do their work. Thank you, Lord, that their honest efforts will be obvious and bring them favor with their supervisors and coworkers. Amen.

SOUND ADVICE

Wisdom is found in those who take advice.

PROVERBS 13:10

Have you ever noticed how helpful it can be to talk with someone about something that is troubling you? God has gifted some of his children with discernment and the ability to be wise counselors. Their sound advice is based on God's Word and on their desire to minister in his name. Their words often point us in new directions or provide new perspectives to old problems. God has gifted us with incomparable counselors. May they hear our thanks as well as our troubles.

CONOVER SWOFFORD

AS YOU PRAY TODAY:

- Thank God for his wondrous care and provision through godly counselors.
- Pray for supernatural discernment as counselors listen to our troubles and lead us to a resolution.
- Ask the Father to give you sound wisdom when someone comes to you for advice.

A MODERN PLAGUE

Comfort, comfort my people, says your God.

ISAIAH 40:1

Reviled, persecuted, taunted, shunned. These are words that describe the biblical treatment of lepers—and words that often describe the treatment of persons diagnosed with HIV, the precursor to AIDS. According to the World Health Organization more than 40 million people are infected with this incurable virus. More than 500,000 of these are children. While once confined to the homosexual community, heterosexual transmission accounts for 80 percent of the spread of HIV/AIDS today.

S.M.H.

AS YOU PRAY TODAY:

- Consider those you may know who have been diagnosed with HIV—ask God to relieve their suffering.
- Ask God to give researchers wisdom as they search for a cure.
- Promiscuous, unprotected sex is the primary transmission of this disease. Pray that our nation returns to a godly standard of sex within the confines of heterosexual marriage.

THE SULTAN'S EXPULSION

God, the blessed and only Ruler, the King of kings and Lord of lords who alone is immortal and who lives in unapproachable light, whom no one has seen or can see. To him be honor and might forever. Amen.

1 Timothy 6:15–16

Brunei occupies a small corner of the Malaysian island of Borneo. A Protectorate of Britain until its independence in 1983, Brunei is now governed by a sultan who declared the nation an Islamic state. Populated by a mix of Malaysians, Chinese, and tribal peoples, Brunei's freedom of religion has been eroded by the sultan's expulsion of all Christian leaders in 1991. Christian literature and contact with Christians in other countries has also been banned.

AS YOU PRAY TODAY:

- Pray for the Sultan of Brunei to meet the King of kings.
- Pray that Brunei students studying at foreign universities will come into contact with godly believers, be won to Christ, and return to their homeland as a witness for the Savior.
- Pray for the evangelization of Brunei's isolated tribal peoples by the few Christian nationals in the country.

FREEDOM'S SONG

If the Son sets you free, you will be free indeed.

John 8:36

O God, to Thee I come today,
And with true repentance kneeling.
The while I bend my knee to pray,
The tears from mine eyes are stealing.
But for Thy grace lost would I be,
Or ship-wrecked on life's hidden shoals,
Or left to drift upon the sea
Where dwelleth all earth's derelict souls.
But Thou didst free from all alarms
And shield me from the tempter's power;
Thou broke the shackles from my arms
And Thou didst cheer my darkest hour.
Thou hast supplied my every need,
And made me free, and free indeed.

Theodore Henry Shackelford

AS YOU PRAY TODAY:

- Imagine what it would be like to be chained and in prison. Then imagine being set free and taken care of by a loving father. Thank God for doing that for you by giving you freedom from sin in Jesus.
- Find a hymn or song that speaks of the freedom we have in Christ. Sing it or read it as a prayer of thanks to God.

ATTENTION!

Search me, O God, and know my heart;
test me and know my anxious thoughts.
See if there is any offensive way in me,
and lead me in the way everlasting.

PSALM 139:23–24

We are careful to straighten our homes so that others may come in and find hospitality. We are fastidious in caring for our clothes and outside appearance, too. But God wants us to pay attention to something more important—our ways. He wants us to look more closely at the deeper parts of our attitudes and our emotions. Have we been harboring grudges? Dwelling on dissatisfaction or envy? Smiley faces and neat haircuts won't cure hearts that are afflicted with bad attitudes. We need to pay attention in order to keep our hearts in line with God's heart.

S.M.H.

AS YOU PRAY TODAY:

- Ask God to show you those heart attitudes that are contrary to his will and ways.
- Ask God's forgiveness for the attitudes that don't reflect his heart.
- Ask for filling of holy contentment, love, and joy.

OBEDIENT CHILDREN

I have no greater joy than to hear that my children are walking in the truth.

3 John 1:4

Return again unto us, O Lord God, we beseech thee. Raise up sons and daughters unto Abraham, and grant that there might come a mighty shaking of dry bones among us, and a great ingathering of souls. Quicken thy professing children. Grant that the young may be constrained to believe that there is a reality in religion, and a beauty in the fear of the Lord. And do thou, Lord, bestow upon them wise and understanding hearts.

Maria W. Stewart

AS YOU PRAY TODAY:

- Pray for the children in your family that they will be obedient to God's will and way in their lives.
- Ask the Lord to use you as an example of faithful obedience to his direction in your own life.
- Thankfully claim God's promises that he wants all children to be saved and to follow him.

MEETING TOGETHER

Jesus said, "By this all men will know that you are my disciples, if you love one another."

JOHN 13:35

A denominational meeting of a major church group was marked by strong words of dissent as delegates deliberated several controversial issues. Reporters from local television stations and newspapers were dispatched to the convention center to interview the spokesmen as they exited the building. Reporters were surprised to find the delegates of the disparate viewpoints laughing over a shared comment. "We may not agree on much," a delegate told the shocked reporters, "but we love each other in the Lord."

S.M.H.

AS YOU PRAY TODAY:

- Remember the upcoming denominational meetings for your church.
- Pray for the delegates who will attend and the agenda that will be discussed.
- Intercede for their witness, that the delegates will remember *Whose* they are and *Who* they represent.

STATESMEN IN THE STATEHOUSE

Daniel was trustworthy and neither corrupt nor negligent.

Daniel 6:4

Patrick Henry, Thomas Jefferson, and Daniel Webster. All served their country in governmental leadership roles. But only one was elected to his state legislature and never served. Though Patrick Henry helped the cause of the American Revolution, drafted the Virginia constitution, and defined our Bill of Rights, Henry died just prior to taking his seat in the Virginia statehouse. Virginia lost a respected statesman that day because Henry not only valued the rights of individuals, he stood firm in his love for God, too.

S.M.H.

AS YOU PRAY TODAY:

- Remember your state representatives. Bring them to God's throne by name.
- Intercede for the decisions they must make, that they will be God-honoring and fair.
- Pray that God will give your state representatives boldness to stand against corruption and vice and become respected statesmen in their statehouse.

A POISONED PARADISE

The mind of sinful man is death, but the mind controlled by the Spirit is life and peace.

ROMANS 8:6

Peaceful palms line the beaches and tea plantations scent the air on the island Sri Lanka. But beneath the peaceful scenery of this Indian Ocean paradise lies a poison of hatred that has brought violent discrimination to ethnic and religious minorities. Though Christians were welcomed in Sri Lanka centuries ago, anti-Christian feeling is on the rise among the large Buddhist majority. Believing that Christianity is a leftover of foreign colonialism, many Sri Lankans are resistant to the Gospel.

AS YOU PRAY TODAY:

- Pray that Sri Lankans will abandon the poison of hate and find the peace of Christ.
- Intercede for those bound by the fear of evil spirits and by ancestor worship.
- Pray for a new generation of workers to bring the Gospel to the less-reached villages of Sri Lanka.

FOUNDED ON THE ROCK

God is the Rock, his works are perfect,
and all his ways are just.

DEUTERONOMY 32:4

Six times in this chapter God is referred to as the "Rock." Throughout the Old Testament God earns this name because of his immovable strength, his sure foundation for our faith and belief. Matthew Henry puts it this way: "God is the rock, for he is in himself immutable, immovable, and he is to all that seek him and fly to him an impenetrable shelter, and to all that trust in him an everlasting foundation."

AS YOU PRAY TODAY:

- Reflect on where you have placed your faith's foundation. Is it on the Rock of God?
- Stand firm on the foundation of God's promises to you—to care for you always.
- Claim him as your solid shelter, one that cannot be overthrown or demolished by the winds or waves of crises.

AMBIDEXTROUS SPIRITUAL WARFARE

[David's soldiers] were armed with bows and were able to shoot arrows or to sling stones right-handed or left-handed.

1 Chronicles 12:2

These warriors were really prepared for battle—able to fight with both hands, if necessary. Most often our battlefields are spiritual battlefields, but do we fight our spiritual battles with both hands, like these warriors, or are we stuck in a rut that uses only one way, one side of our faith, to fight the enemy? Do we try use our own strengths, ideas and words to fight evil? Paul says that "the weapons we fight with are not the weapons of the world. On the contrary, they have divine power to demolish strongholds" (2 Corinthians 10:4). We need to ask God for his weapons and throw our own aside. Our weapons are flimsy, but God's are powerful!

S.M.H.

AS YOU PRAY TODAY:

- Claim God's power to pull down the strongholds in your life.
- Pray for forgiveness for holding bad feelings against someone else. This is a stronghold.
- Pray for a healing of the hurt that someone's rejection has caused you. This is a stronghold, too.

REAPING POSITIVE FRUIT

The one who sows to please his sinful nature, from that nature will reap destruction; the one who sows to please the Spirit, from the Spirit will reap eternal life.

GALATIANS 6:8

We know the truth of the principle that we will reap what we sow. Farmers' fields attest to that fact every season. But let's add another dimension to this principle: The way we act impacts other peoples' lives. If our example to unsaved friends reflects disobedience to God's ways, it would be ludicrous to expect that their response to the Gospel would be positive. It is only as our witness reflects God's life-changing power that we can reap the positive fruit of bringing unsaved friends to Christ.

S.M.H.

AS YOU PRAY TODAY:

- Ask God to help you to be a positive witness for him to your unsaved friends.
- Pray for an opportunity to share spiritual things with them.
- Ask God to open your unsaved friends' hearts to the Gospel message.

CARE FOR THE DYING

Though I walk through the valley
of the shadow of death,
I will fear no evil,
for you are with me, O Lord.

PSALM 23:4

One of the blessings of a terminal illness spent at home is that it gives the dying person time to reflect on his life, to make peace, to ask forgiveness if necessary, and to say good-by to loved ones. Hospice, by supporting families who care for the dying at home, has allowed many to experience a "good death." Hospice is most often a system of home care, supported by a team of doctors, nurses, health aides, social workers, and volunteers. The whole family, not just the patient, is the unit of care.

BARBARA DEANE

AS YOU PRAY TODAY:

- Pray for hospice workers in your area. Caring for the dying is physically and emotionally tiring work.
- Pray for the patients and families involved in hospice care programs. Patients usually have less than six months to live.

PRAY AS YOU PASS

Show proper respect to everyone.

1 PETER 2:17

According to a recent survey, teasing by peers and the pressure for grades ranked lowest in the concerns of 5,000 school age children. Issues about violence placed near the top, but the greatest concern for these children was the problem of student discipline. With many students showing no respect for their teachers, schools are becoming volatile places. Prayer cover on our nation's schools is desperately needed so that all our students will feel safe as they learn.

S.M.H.

AS YOU PRAY TODAY:

- As you pass neighborhood schools today, pray for relationships between teachers and students.
- Petition God to restore a respect of authority by providing teachers who respect children and themselves enough to demand it.
- Ask God to open opportunities for you to serve in your local school—as an aide, volunteer, or committee member.

A NEW SAVIOR FOR ROMANIA

There is no God apart from me, a righteous God and a Savior; there is none but me.

Isaiah 45:21

For twenty-four years, Nicolae Ceausescu ruled Romania with an iron fist. The friendly people and beautiful countryside withered under the cruel tyranny of this Communist dictator who referred to himself as the Sacred Word, Savior, and Chosen One. Christians were routinely persecuted or jailed, and many were killed. When Ceausescu was overthrown by a national rebellion in 1989, the Gospel began to be preached openly. Many Romanians are today learning about a "new" Savior—a heavenly One.

AS YOU PRAY TODAY:

- Pray that God will raise leaders in Romania that will rule wisely and fairly.
- Praise God for the positive response of the Romanian people to the Gospel message.
- Ask God to send godly workers to Romania to help care for abandoned children and the elderly.

ELOHIM

I am the LORD, and there is no other;
apart from me there is no God.

ISAIAH 45:5

Satan challenges and counterfeits everything that God is. If the enemy of our souls can convince us that we are the master of anything—finances, families, careers, home—then we could also believe that we could master our selves . . . we wouldn't need a Savior. Yet Scripture unravels this lie. Isaiah tells us that God is the only God—not us, not our careers, not even our credit cards. Our hearts should be emblazoned with the T-shirt message: There is only one God . . . and you are not Him!

S.M.H.

AS YOU PRAY TODAY:

- Ask God to reveal any hidden areas in your life where you have taken over God's place as god.
- Confess your acceptance of Satan's lie that you can be God.
- Relinquish control of your life, and all that it entails, and let God be God.

FINDING FAVOR

Whatever you do, work at it with all your heart, as working for the Lord, not for men, since you know that you will receive an inheritance from the Lord as a reward.

COLOSSIANS 3:23–24

Sometimes you find there's more to a profession than meets the eye. "It's not my job, man," was a recurring comment made by the leading character in a 1980s sitcom. Those who live by his assertion may object to requests that fall in a job description's gray area of "other related duties." Yet God has given us our job, and we should do it with gusto and for his glory. Our bosses will notice our enthusiasm, and our job will become an opportunity to spread God's love to others. Jesus found favor with God and man. We can find favor with our employers, too, by the way we handle those "other related duties."

S.M.H.

AS YOU PRAY TODAY:

- Be thankful for your job.
- Pray for your boss to make right decisions.
- Praise God for the opportunity to honor him in your work.

ASK AND RECEIVE

Whatever you ask for in prayer, believe that you have received it, and it will be yours.

MARK 11:24

God has given you His promise
That He hears and answers prayer.
He will heed your supplication
If you cast on Him your care.
He will answer every prayer,
He will answer every prayer,
Go to Him in faith believing,
He will answer every prayer.
He will not withhold one blessing,
He will give you what is best.
God will answer by His Spirit,
Every one who makes request.

AS YOU PRAY TODAY:

- Begin your prayer with thanksgiving that God hears and answers all your prayers.
- Pray boldly for all of your concerns, as you would ask a loving father for the things you need.

MORE THAN A BUILDING

In Christ the whole building is joined together and rises to become a holy temple in the Lord.

EPHESIANS 2:21

We dedicate this house unto thee, O, thou that dwellest in heaven. Receive it, O, receive it, among thine earthly sanctuaries, and grant that all who may worship thee here, from Sabbath to Sabbath, and from generation to generation, even our children's children, may feel it to be indeed the house of God, and the gate of heaven! Amen.

DANIEL ALEXANDER PAYNE

AS YOU PRAY TODAY:

- Take note of the church buildings in your neighborhood and pray for each congregation that meets there.
- Invoke God's blessing on those sanctuaries that they will be used in ways that will glorify him.
- Intercede for those congregations that they will enfold the community in the light of God's love.

BABIES HAVING BABIES

Do not arouse or awaken love until it so desires.

SONG OF SONGS 8:4

On the way to work she saw her—a teenager, holding a tiny, wiggly bundle. A baby. And her heart ached. Another baby having a baby. Another young woman seeking her worth through peer pressure and passion. Another new life who would probably never know a stable family environment. And she wondered, where was the young man who was responsible for fathering this sweet, wiggly one? Had no one stood by him to help him withstand the taunts to "be a man"? Who failed these teens, anyway? And she drove on, condemning herself by her silence.

S.M.H.

AS YOU PRAY TODAY:

- Open your heart to the hurt God feels for the growing number of teenage pregnancies.
- Remember the teens in your life and pray for their courage and sexual purity.
- Ask God to give you an opportunity to share his views on sex with a child you love.

DRY AND DUSTY DJIBOUTI

"Those who seek me find me," says the Lord.

PROVERBS 8:17

Just above the horn of Africa is the crescent-shaped nation of Djibouti. Plagued by drought and limited by lack of industry or natural resources, Djibouti is one of the few Muslim nations in Africa that allows open evangelical witness for Christ. The Afars and Somalis make up the largest people groups in the country. Both groups like to learn, so missionaries offer classes in the Christian bookstore in English and French using the Christian books from the store as their textbooks.

AS YOU PRAY TODAY:

- Praise God for the opportunities to share the Gospel in Djibouti. Pray that this openness will continue.
- Pray for the leaders of Djibouti's government, that they will have the wisdom to unite the Afars and Somalis.
- Ask God to send long-term missionaries to work with refugees from neighboring Somalia and Ethiopia.

THE GOD OF ETERNITY

God has also set eternity in the hearts of men; yet they cannot fathom what God has done from beginning to end.

ECCLESIASTES 3:11

We cannot grasp eternity, but we can learn something of it by perceiving that whatever portion of time we consider, eternity is vaster than the vastest. Yet, all that eternity, magnificent as it is, never was without an Inhabitant. God's dwelling place is that eternity which has neither past nor future. It is one vast, immeasurable present. And that, brethren, is the inward seal with which God has stamped himself upon man's heart.

FREDERICK W. ROBERTSON

AS YOU PRAY TODAY:

- Know absolutely that God is greater than time and greater than your moment of joy or pain.
- Contemplate God's greatness that allows him to see past, present, and future all at once.
- Sense the seed of eternity placed in your own heart. Trust him to take care of your future needs, plans, and desires.

A SEAT AT HIS FEET

"Martha, Martha," the Lord answered, "you are worried and upset about many things, but only one thing is needed. Mary has chosen what is better, and it will not be taken away from her."

LUKE 10:41–42

Ministry for Jesus can become a weight we drag around. We become so busy *for* him, we don't have time to be *with* him. When Mary was seated at the feet of the Lord, Martha was busy in the kitchen. Jesus looked at Martha and said [essentially], "If you spend time waiting upon me, seated at my feet, it puts something in you. You will not only look good, but you'll also be good for something." We must wait in his presence and allow all ministry to be born of relationship.

DUTCH SHEETS

AS YOU PRAY TODAY:

- Take time to listen to God's answers when you pray today.
- Find solace in sitting at Jesus' feet.
- Pray that whatever involves your time and energy will be good, profitable, and useful to God and others.

TALK TO ME!

If anyone speaks, he should do it as one speaking the very words of God.

1 PETER 4:11

God communicates with his children in different ways. With Moses, David, and Ezekiel, God spoke his word directly to them. With unbelieving Israel, God used signs and wonders to communicate. And with still others, God's written Word touched their hearts.

We need to use God's communication styles in our families, too. Written notes might work better than lecturing a teenager. A favorite meal could signal "Congratulations." A quiet conversation may be needed to solve a problem. By talking with our family like God talks to us, we can better communicate how much we love each other.

S.M.H.

AS YOU PRAY TODAY:

- Ask God to show you the best way to communicate with your family.
- Ask him for courage to try these new ways to communicate.
- Pray that God reminds you that good communication always begins with good listening skills.

YOU CAN BANK ON IT

Do not forget to do good and to share with others, for with such sacrifices God is pleased.

HEBREWS 13:16

Soup kitchens came into prominence in America during the Great Depression. With millions out of work, churches and charitable organizations opened their doors to give the unemployed a warm meal. Soon, this practice was expanded to include the distribution of free food to families in need. Today, many communities maintain a food pantry where struggling families can receive supplemental groceries at little or no cost. Corporations donate some of this food, but most likely your food bank can consistently provide for others because of the generosity of folks like you.

S.M.H.

AS YOU PRAY TODAY:

- Ask God to encourage people to generously donate to your food bank.
- Pray for the leaders of your local food pantry—for wisdom, compassion, and integrity.
- Pray for the families who will receive the food—for strength, health, and a job, if needed.

PRAYERS FOR UNWED MOTHERS

A father to the fatherless, a defender of widows, is God in his holy dwelling.

PSALM 68:5

In the 1950s, most single parent households were composed of widows. Today they are composed primarily of divorcees and unwed mothers. Most of these unwed mothers are trapped in the cycle of poverty and government assistance. Their children are absent from school more frequently and are more likely to repeat a grade, to require remedial education, and to be referred to a psychologist than children from two-parent homes. Unwed mothers and their children are in need of God's love, and his grace. They also need our prayers.

S.M.H.

AS YOU PRAY TODAY:

- Let God bring to mind an unwed mother from your family, church, or community. Pray for her by name.
- Praise God for Christ-focused programs that counsel unwed mothers and their children.
- Pray that extended family members will come alongside unwed mothers with prayers, encouragement, and love.

THE LAND OF THE BLACK EAGLE

Seek the LORD while he may be found; call on him while he is near.

ISAIAH 55:6

In 1944 Albania became a Communist country and for the next forty-one years was isolated from the rest of the world. Albanians survived with very little food, supplies, and modern materials. Religious books and meetings were banned, and it was against the law to pray. But when Albania's ruler died in 1991, the Communist government fell. The black eagle that flies on the Albanian flag now flies over a democratic republic that is once again open to the Gospel.

AS YOU PRAY TODAY:

- Praise God for the spectacular changes in Albania—from an atheist dictatorship to a free democracy.
- Pray against the discriminatory religious practices that Muslim extremists are promoting.
- Regularly ask God to strengthen new believers and to encourage them to share their faith with others.

MAKE ME LIKE YOU

Be made new in the attitude of your minds; and . . . put on the new self, created to be like God in true righteousness and holiness.

EPHESIANS 4:23–24

Make me a heart gentle and humble,
loving without asking any return,
large-hearted and undauntable,
which no ingratitude can sour
and no indifference can weary;
a heart penetrated by the love of Jesus
whose desire will only be satisfied in heaven.
Grant me, O Lord,
the mind and heart
of thy dear Son.

TRANSLATED FROM THE FRENCH BY GEORGE APPLETON

AS YOU PRAY TODAY:

- Rejoice in God's promise to mold us into his character.
- Pray for a deeper, fuller understanding of God's nature and his desire for your life.
- Ask God to transform your thoughts, ways, and words to make you more like him.

HINDERED PRAYERS

I want men everywhere to lift up holy hands in prayer.

1 TIMOTHY 2:8

There are prayers which are unanswered because they are hindered. Some day they may be answered, but for a time they are held up by some obstacle. Heavy snows hold up morning traffic. But when colliding cars are hauled away and the snow-plow gets through, the flow of traffic goes on.

Is there an obstacle which may hinder our prayers? Resentment and unforgiveness are the roots of many diseases from which people suffer intensely. To be unforgiving is rebellion against God. And this is sin. Sin hinders one's prayers from being answered.

ROSALIND RINKER

AS YOU PRAY TODAY:

- Ask God to search your heart and illumine every part.
- Release any harbored grudges you may be holding against another.
- Confess any resentment you feel toward anyone and seek God's forgiveness.

INTERRUPTIONS OR OPPORTUNITIES

Teach us to number our days aright, O Lord,
that we may gain a heart of wisdom.

PSALM 90:12

We begin our week, committing each day to the Lord, recognizing that he is in charge of our lives. So we begin to put the pieces of our day together, but then the phone rings, or the doorbell chimes, and our plans fly out the window. Once again our friends or family have interrupted our plans. Depending on how busy we are, those interruptions can be quite bothersome. But stop and think. If God is in control of our time, couldn't it be that what we view as interruptions are actually God's opportunities . . . to minister, to listen, to love?

S.M.H.

AS YOU PRAY TODAY:

- Ask God to open your eyes to opportunities in the interruptions to your schedule.
- Ask God's forgiveness for the resentment that surfaces when your schedule is interrupted.
- Pray for his eyes of compassion as these interruptions come your way.

'DOPTED!

God predestined us to be adopted as his sons through Jesus Christ, in accordance with his pleasure and will—to the praise of his glorious grace, which he has freely given us in the One he loves.

EPHESIANS 1:5–6

Dinnertime is punctuated with boisterous conversation. The house is full of love. Very full, in fact, for twelve adopted children live here.

When Cathy and Stan adopted their first child sixteen years ago, little did they know they would become parents to children of all ages, from all over the world, with special needs. But ask two-year-old Carrie what the best thing is about her family and she'll tell you, "They love me. They chose me. I'm 'dopted!"

S.M.H.

AS YOU PRAY TODAY:

- Pray for adoption agencies seeking to place children in loving homes.
- Pray for overwhelming patience as adoptive parents and families go through the adoption process.
- Pray for adoptive families as they adjust to new faces, new ways, and new family members.

THE JURISDICTION OF A JUSTICE

Let justice roll on like a river, righteousness like a never-failing stream!

AMOS 5:24

Justices of the peace are known for solemnizing wedding vows, but they perform other valuable services for their community, too. Individual states can determine the extent of the jurisdiction of a justice of the peace. Some states allow these magistrates to try only misdemeanors; some states limit their judicial powers to filing civil or criminal cases; and other states grant a justice of the peace authority to try minor criminal cases and civil disputes involving less than $300.

S.M.H.

AS YOU PRAY TODAY:

- Pray for godly wisdom for these magistrates as they perform their duties.
- Ask God to make each justice aware of the solemnity of the wedding ceremonies they perform.
- Pray that the men and women elected to these positions will honor their office with integrity, accountability, and justice.

PNG

Acknowledge . . . God, . . . and serve him with wholehearted devotion and with a willing mind, for the LORD searches every heart and understands every motive behind the thoughts. If you seek him, he will be found by you.

1 CHRONICLES 28:9

Papua New Guinea, otherwise known as PNG, takes up half of the world's second largest island. Thousands of missionaries have gone to this jungle land just north of Australia. Several were martyred by cannibals, but many more survived and translated the Bible into local languages so that nearly every tribe could learn about Jesus. Many villagers have become Christians. But their commitment to Christ is halfhearted. Many have blended their Christianity with witchcraft and spirit worship. Many still fear the curse of sorcerers and witch doctors.

AS YOU PRAY TODAY:

- Pray that believers will live lives that please God and honor him.
- Ask God to set people free from the power of witchcraft and evil spirits.
- Pray that more translators will come to PNG to help finish the work of Bible translation.

A GLORIOUS REDEEMER

All mankind will know that I, the LORD, am your Savior, your Redeemer, the Mighty One of Jacob.

ISAIAH 49:26

Blessed are you, O Lord, for loving me.
Find in my heart continual praise for your compassion.
Blessed are you, O Lord, for paying the penalty for my sin.
Find in my being remorse for my transgression.
Blessed are you, O Lord, for redeeming me from my sinful self.
Find in my spirit acceptance of your atonement.
Blessed are you, O gracious Lord, for all you have done.
Find in my soul abandonment to your will.
All honor, majesty, and praise to my glorious Redeemer. Amen.

S.M.H.

AS YOU PRAY TODAY:

- Rejoice in the mercy of your gracious Redeemer. He has given you forgiveness for the past.
- Rejoice in the love of your glorious Redeemer. He has given you a hope for the future.
- Rejoice in the blessing of your generous Redeemer. He has given you his best for this day.

PREPARED TO DO YOUR WILL

Tuck your cloak into your belt. . . .
Then open the door and run!

2 KINGS 9:1, 3

God was displeased with King Joram of Israel. So God told Elisha to send a spokesman on a dangerous mission . . . run in, secretly anoint Jehu as the new king, and run out. But the messenger had to be tucked in and prepared to run long before he needed to. Why? Maybe someone would have grabbed his flowing robe before he got to Jehu. Maybe he would have stumbled as he ran out. Whatever the reason, the lesson is clear. Being prepared to do God's will is just as important as doing it. Are you prepared to follow God's direction in your life?

S.M.H.

AS YOU PRAY TODAY:

- Indicate your willingness to follow God's will for your life.
- Ask God to show you how you should prepare yourself for God's plan for your life.
- Pray for the strength to follow through on what God shows you.

FRIENDS LIKE YOU

Hushai the Arkite was the king's friend.

1 CHRONICLES 27:33

Tucked into a list of long-forgotten, faceless names is a marvelous verse. Many people rush over it, yet it contains the name of a man who was important to the king and to God. He was a friend—one who listens, keeps secrets, offers a helping hand, comforts, and cares—even if it means danger, even if it involves inconvenience, even if it means sacrifice. Hushai was willing to risk his own life to keep David on the throne. Scripture says that the Lord is our friend, too, and that he sticks closer than a brother. We all need friends—friends like Hushai. Friends like the Lord. Friends like you.

S.M.H.

AS YOU PRAY TODAY:

- Pray that the Lord will provide you with good friends like Hushai.
- Ask the Lord to make you more like himself—a friend to those around you.
- Commit to praying for your friends in every spare moment of this day.

THE AFTER SCHOOL GOSPEL GROUP

Jesus said, "Let the little children come to me, and do not hinder them, for the kingdom of heaven belongs to such as these."

MATTHEW 19:14

Backyard Bible clubs, vacation Bible schools, Campus Life clubs—all of these after-school activities share the Gospel with children in different ways. Some meet on school campuses, some gather at churches, and still others are held in neighborhood homes and backyards across the nation. But in all of these activities, kids learn about a personal relationship with Jesus. All of these fulfill Jesus' call in Matthew 19:14.

S.M.H.

AS YOU PRAY TODAY:

- Pray God's blessing on the after-school ministries in your area—for teachers, students, and helpers.
- Ask God to stir hearts to give of their time and money to support these outreaches.
- Pray that God will give the leaders of these outreach ministries a Christ-focused life, a hunger for his Word, and a desire to see souls saved.

LIGHTHOUSES OF THE AIR

Their voice goes out into all the earth, their words to the ends of the world.

PSALM 19:4

In our mobile society many of us spend hours in our cars listening to the radio as we commute to work. Sometimes we'll turn on the radio while sunning by the swimming pool or working on household tasks. Though different types of radio programming are available in most localities, some areas may have only one Christian radio station. These lighthouses of the airwaves offer everything from Christian music to Bible teaching. God's message reaches many through the ministry of this medium.

S.M.H.

AS YOU PRAY TODAY:

- Rejoice that you live in a society that allows the free broadcast of the Gospel.
- Pray that God will provide generous support for Christian broadcasting in both money and personnel.
- Ask God to give your station managers wisdom as they plan their broadcast schedules. May the material and music bring many to Christ.

ECUADOR'S FORGOTTEN ONES

God will defend the afflicted among the people and save the children of the needy.

PSALM 72:4

You see them on the well-worn, two-foot-wide median that divides the city's busiest street. Vehicles zip past at alarming speeds while these preschoolers play tag, oblivious to the danger. But when the traffic halts, these little ones press their dirty faces against closed car windows, begging for pennies. At night older children join them and spit gasoline into the air, lit by matches into flaming, dragon-like plumes, hoping for a coin from a passing motorist. These are Ecuador's forgotten ones: slum-dwelling children with no hope for a future.

AS YOU PRAY TODAY:

- Few Christian workers have a vision for these children. Pray that God will stir hearts.
- Pray that God will give these children godly mentors to a good future outside the slums.
- Ask God to bless those who minister among the "fire blowers." May they be able to find gainful employment for these children.

DIVINE HOPE

Put your hope in God, for I will yet praise him, my Savior and my God.

PSALM 43:5

What need there is that up out of this darkness and trouble and sadness, out of these calamities, there should be exalted, somewhere, an image that brings God right home to man's need. The world would die if it had no hope of finding such a God. He penetrates and pervades the world with more saving mercies than does the sun with particles of light and heat. He declares that his nature in himself is boundless—that his work of comfort is endless.

HENRY WARD BEECHER

AS YOU PRAY TODAY:

- Thank God for difficult times that make us aware of our need for God.
- Praise him for his tender thoughts and actions for you, his child.
- Rejoice that God's heart of mercy is inexhaustible.

LET US ADORE HIM

Worthy is the Lamb, who was slain, to receive power and wealth and wisdom and strength and honor and glory and praise!

REVELATION 5:12

O most high, how great is my dilemma! In your awful presence silence seems best. And yet, if I keep my peace, the rocks themselves will cry out. But if I do speak, what will I say?

It is Love that calls forth my speech, though it still feels like stammering. I adore you. I worship you. I magnify you, Lord. Let me see your greatness—to the extent that I can receive it. Help me bow in your presence in endless wonder and ceaseless praise.

In the name of him whose adoration never fails. Amen.

RICHARD FOSTER

AS YOU PRAY TODAY:

- Thank God for his gifts of grace and mercy.
- Praise him for the joy of his presence, the beauty of his creation, and the blessing of family and friends.

GLORY, SEEK, REJOICE, & LOOK

Glory in his holy name; let the hearts of those who seek the LORD rejoice. Look to the LORD and his strength.

1 CHRONICLES 16:10–11

Simple commands . . . glory, seek, rejoice, look . . . yet difficult for self-sufficient people. They mean leaving things in God's hands, not running after our own plans. There's an order to these commands, too. First we must remember God's faithfulness, his care and provision. How else could we glory in his name? After remembering, we can seek his face and rejoice. Finally, we can look about us with a secure knowledge of God's strength and power. What a formula to start each day: glory, seek, rejoice, and look!

S.M.H.

AS YOU PRAY TODAY:

- Pray that your friends will remember all that God has done for them.
- Pray that they will come into his presence with rejoicing.
- Look into the future and see God's strength standing ready to come to your friends' aid. Hallelujah!

THROUGH THE BIBLE

All Scripture is God-breathed and is useful for teaching, rebuking, correcting and training in righteousness, so that the man of God may be thoroughly equipped for every good work.

2 TIMOTHY 3:16–17

When Dr. W. A. Criswell first came to the First Baptist Church of Dallas, Texas, he announced that he would preach through the Bible. He made it in seventeen years and eight months. At first the church members were fearful it would wreck the church, but the opposite happened. Hundreds and hundreds joined. Converts used to say, "I joined in Isaiah," or "I joined in 1 Timothy." Is the study of Scripture a priority in your life and church?

AS YOU PRAY TODAY:

- Pray for those who teach Bible study classes in your church—for guidance and inspiration.
- Ask God to kindle a hunger in your own heart for Bible study.
- Seek God's direction on ways that you can help start a Bible study in your home, neighborhood, or church.

A SILENT SHAME

Philip ran up to the chariot and heard the man reading Isaiah the prophet. "Do you understand what you are reading?" Philip asked. "How can I," he said, "unless someone explains it to me?" So he invited Philip to come up and sit with him.

ACTS 8:30–31

Jim's secret was out. His wife had asked him to read his grandson a storybook at bedtime. Jim usually made all kinds of excuses when it came to reading aloud. But tonight he realized that the only way he could overcome his silent shame was with the courageous confession, "I can't read."

Former First Lady Barbara Bush believes that literacy can curb many of our social ills. Through her Foundation for Family Literacy, reading programs throughout the United States find support. Could you find some time to be a reading tutor for someone like Jim?

S.M.H.

AS YOU PRAY TODAY:

- Pray that God will send many reading tutor volunteers to illiteracy programs in your community.

JUST BEING THERE

When you walk through the fire, you will not be burned;
the flames will not set you ablaze.

ISAIAH 43:2

Several men tried to break into a missionary's home near Nairobi, Kenya. Henry, a security guard, stopped them, but was viciously attacked during the scuffle. While another guard called a doctor, the missionary came out of the house and held Henry in his arms, staunching blood flowing from a gash in Henry's head. Henry later thanked the missionary saying, "Thank you, Bwana, for being there for me."

Though messages and programs help communicate the Gospel, it is often the presence of a missionary and their interaction with the local people that best illustrates the truth of God's love.

ADAPTED FROM RANDY WEST

AS YOU PRAY TODAY:

- Ask God to send more caring missionaries like Henry's friend to the people of Kenya.
- Pray that God will remind his servants to look beyond programs to the people they serve.

GOD'S EXPECTATIONS

What does the LORD require of you? To act justly and to love mercy and to walk humbly with your God.

MICAH 6:8

Advertising agencies tell us what we should buy, wear, and think. Well-meaning friends suggest we do this or that. We can feel pulled in many directions. Yet the Bible is quite clear about God's expectations: we should show justice and mercy to others.

Doing what God expects sets the God-seekers apart from the self-seekers. Few people opt to care for others because it is easier not to. But when we follow God's expectations, we show something to others that they need to see: God's love alive in us.

S.M.H.

AS YOU PRAY TODAY:

- Ask God to let his nature flow through you.
- Pray that justice and mercy will become second nature to you, too.
- Desire to be more God-seeking than self-seeking and thereby show God's kingdom to others.

A SERVANT'S PLACE

Moses was faithful as a servant in all God's house.

HEBREWS 3:5

The Lord uses all of us in different ways. We may complain that we don't have the same talents as another, but the Lord has a place of service for all of us that is uniquely fitted to our particular abilities. Moses began his service for God reluctantly. He claimed that he lacked the skills to do what God wanted him to do. But God refused to accept Moses' excuses and provided him with tools to complete the task. In the wilderness, God fitted Moses for service, to lead Israel out of captivity. For what service has he fitted you?

S.M.H.

AS YOU PRAY TODAY:

- Ask God to clearly show you your gifts and abilities.
- Pray for an opportunity to use those gifts for his glory.
- Acknowledge your dependence on God to supply you with the provisions needed to serve him in this way.

FIGHTING THE RIGHT BATTLE

We have different gifts, according to the grace given us.

ROMANS 12:6

God has created one being and one unity with this intent, that each one in fulfilling his ministry shall do the work allotted to him. Therefore let every man fight the good fight in his own calling. If you are a man or woman and say to yourself: I will fulfill my ministry; I will do the work which God has given me and seek no other, you are fighting the right battle. You have your calling from God.

MARTIN LUTHER

AS YOU PRAY TODAY:

- Remember the talents and abilities that God has given your spouse. Pray that God will use these for his honor.
- Seek the calling God has set aside for your children. Pray that God will use them for his glory.
- Bring your brothers and sisters to the Lord. Intercede for each one to fulfill the ministry God has given them.

FIVE HUNDRED LANDLORDS

A wife of noble character who can find?
She is worth far more than rubies.

PROVERBS 31:10

Katie's mom is like most moms. She makes supper and cleans the house. She gets her kids to school on time and tucks them into bed at night.

But Katie's home is different. Katie's home has 500 landlords. That's because Katie's mom is a pastor's wife. Every church member has an opinion about how Katie's mom should maintain the parsonage and where she should spend her time.

The greatest gift you can show your pastor and his family is to offer your friendship and love. Showing your appreciation with small acts of kindness will mean the world to them.

S.M.H.

AS YOU PRAY TODAY:

- Thank God for your pastor's family. They are his refuge.
- Reflect on your attitudes toward your pastor's wife. Is she a friend or just an employee of the church? She doesn't need another job, but she probably could use the friendship.

GOOD SAMARITANS

A man . . . fell into the hands of robbers. They stripped him of his clothes, beat him and went away, leaving him half dead . . . A Samaritan, as he traveled, came where the man was; and when he saw him, he took pity on him.

LUKE 10:30, 33

Hurrying to an appointment, a father quickly ushered his daughter past a man who had fallen and cut his head. When she asked why they hadn't stopped to help, the father replied that the man was drunk. The child persisted saying, "Daddy, the Good Samaritan would have stopped." Her comment stirred the father to action. Strangely enough, the fellow wasn't drunk—he was having a seizure and needed immediate medical attention.

Many times we rush past accident victims and stranded motorists in a hurry. Yet we may be the only lifeline those folks have.

S.M.H.

AS YOU PRAY TODAY:

- If you can't stop, ask God to send help to accident victims or stranded motorists that you see today.
- Pray for wisdom to know if you are God's intended Good Samaritan in this situation.

A PACIFIC PARADISE

God establishes justice on earth. In his law the islands will put their hope.

ISAIAH 42:4

The islands of Fiji lie in the Pacific Ocean off the eastern shores of Australia. Largely Christianized, the Fijian people are almost outnumbered by immigrants from India who came decades ago to work in Fiji's sugar cane fields. Disturbed by the inroads that Muslim, Hindu, and Sikh Indians were making into the Fijian government, some Fijian Christians began persecuting others with different religious beliefs, setting fire to mosques and Hindu temples.

AS YOU PRAY TODAY:

- Pray that the Fijian government will be fair to all people and allow godly principles to reign in their country.
- Pray that Fijian believers will treat outsiders with love and kindness so that their witness will not be in vain.
- Ask God to renew the Fijian's missionary vigor to show others God's love and power.

THE CROSS OF CHRIST

Christ gave himself for our sins to rescue us.

GALATIANS 1:4

The cross makes us whole; not all at once indeed, but it does the work effectually. Before we reached it we were broken and scattered, without a center toward which to gravitate. The cross forms that center, and draws together the disordered fragments of our being; producing a wholeness of unity that no object of less powerful attractiveness could accomplish: a wholeness or unity that, beginning with the individual, reproduces itself on a larger scale in God's holy church.

HORATIUS BONAR

AS YOU PRAY TODAY:

- Have you found your way to the cross of Christ? If so, rejoice in the eternal blessing of everlasting life. If not, come today and receive God's greatest gift.
- Weep with remembrance at the price your sins cost Christ. Thank him for his sacrifice.
- Praise God for the spiritual healing available to you in the cross.

FAITHFUL IN OUR FRUIT

The fruit of the Spirit is love, joy, peace, patience, kindness, goodness, faithfulness, gentleness and self-control.

GALATIANS 5:22–23

King Joash produced righteous fruit. Crowned as king of Judah when he was seven years old, Joash followed God's laws by listening to the advice of godly leaders. Sometimes it seems that we grow only crops of frustration, anger, and selfishness rather than producing fruit of kindness, love, and trust. Why? Maybe Joash did a better job of listening to the advice of godly friends. Maybe Joash spent more time close to God. Whatever the reason, if a seven-year-old can produce righteous fruit, we should be able to, too.

S.M.H.

AS YOU PRAY TODAY:

- Ask God to break up the ground of your heart to sense the bad seeds of sin before they sprout and become ingrained.
- Claim God's wisdom in all your steps today.
- Pray for a crop of righteousness as you spend more time with God in prayer and Bible study.

HABITUAL LIVING

If anyone is in Christ, he is a new creation; the old has gone, the new has come!

2 CORINTHIANS 5:17

We've often watched our close friends do things we know are not good for them. It may be a simple matter of biting their fingernails or a major infraction like driving while intoxicated. Our friends excuse these actions in all sorts of ways. But there comes a time when we all should be done with old habits and start building new ones. It is never easy, but God has promised to help us. God may just have put you in your friends' life to encourage them and pray them through these bad habits, too.

CONOVER SWOFFORD

AS YOU PRAY TODAY:

- Pray that God will convict your friends of their harmful habits.
- Ask God to show you what you can do to help your friend in their struggle with bad habits.
- Thank God for giving your friend release from the bondage of sinful habits.

THE WISDOM OF THE AGED

Is not wisdom found among the aged?
Does not long life bring understanding?

JOB 12:12

Today's society maintains that all members of society have a stake in raising the children of that society. To take that one step further, all members of a society have a responsibility to the aged of that society. In many parts of the world, we relegate the aged to nursing facilities and visit when it's convenient. Yet the Bible reminds us that our elders are a resource we can't throw away. They are people to be loved, honored and cared for—people who can impart great wisdom if we take the time to listen. In our global village, we need to show respect for the elderly by taking time to be with them and learn from them.

S.M.H.

AS YOU PRAY TODAY:

- Pray for wisdom for the administrators of the nursing homes you drive past today.
- Ask God to direct you to someone in a nursing home who is lonely. Visit him or her this week.

A GUIDING LIGHT

Your word is truth, O God.

JOHN 17:17

In communities across the nation a guiding light shines in the marketplace. That light comes from your local Christian bookstore. Offering Bibles, books, music, and gift items that glorify God, these Christian bookstores are unique in their focus. Every Christian bookstore needs to be run as a good business, but it also seeks to minister to the hearts of its customers. While you may be able to buy a Bible in any bookstore, you'll find more than just good books inside your Christian bookstore.

S.M.H.

AS YOU PRAY TODAY:

- Pray for the ministry of Christian retailers in your community. In many cities, these stores receive hate mail and threatening phone calls.
- Ask God to bless each item that leaves a Christian bookstore, that God's Word will minister to the one using it.
- Pray for a way to encourage your local Christian retailer—maybe with a note or a personal thank you.

LIVING WATER FOR A DRY LAND

All over the world this gospel is bearing fruit and growing.

COLOSSIANS 1:6

Rapid church growth in Chad during the 1960s and 1970s has dried up, just like the lakes in this central African land. War, famine, and poverty have slowed the spread of the Gospel, while legalism and lack of biblical teaching have sapped the strength of existing churches. Muslim and animist beliefs have been mixed with Christianity, too, further watering down the Gospel's impact. Lack of rain and infertile soil make Chad one of the world's poorest countries. This dry land is in desperate need of God's living water.

AS YOU PRAY TODAY:

- Petition God to send rain to fill lakes and provide water for thirsty people and animals.
- Pray that God will send translators to bring the Bible to Chad's more than one hundred language groups.
- Ask God to send missionaries who can strengthen failing churches and evangelize unreached parts of the country.

PREVAILING PRAYER

The prayer of a righteous man is powerful and effective.

JAMES 5:16

The great need of our world, our nation, and our churches is people who know how to prevail in prayer. Moments of pious wishes blandly expressed to God once or twice a day will bring little change on earth. Intercession is more than occasional heart-warming, emotional love to God, more than expressions of good will on our knees when we think of the sick and the suffering among our friends. Prevailing prayer is holy work. Prayer was never meant to be incidental to the work of God. It is the work.

WESLEY L. DUEWEL

AS YOU PRAY TODAY:

- Ask God to show you those things that distract you from prayer time or hunger for him.
- Pray about those things that God places on your heart until heaven's powers are released. Don't give up.

WELL PLEASING

Offer your bodies as living sacrifices, holy and pleasing to God—this is your spiritual act of worship.

ROMANS 12:1

Sins are all around us, wrapped in the popular beliefs of the day that are ignorant of God's standards. Yet to be holy and acceptable to God we need to break free from these sins. We need to value God's values, keep promises, regard the needs of others as important as our own, and consistently, obediently, and dutifully live by God's design. Others may avoid consequences and ignore promises, but those who wish to be pleasing to God need to be distinctively set apart to Christ.

S.M.H.

AS YOU PRAY TODAY:

- Think of yourself as a willing sacrifice, bound and given over to God. Verbalize that commitment.
- Ask God to search your heart and illumine those areas that are not pleasing to him.
- Praise him for his cleansing power that can set you apart and keep you holy.

BAD COMPANIONS

He who walks with the wise grows wise.

PROVERBS 13:20

I want to teach my children how to choose good friends, but I need your wisdom, Lord. Show me how to be a fair judge of character. Help me to know when to let my children make their own decisions about their companions and when I should intervene. Open my children's eyes to the truth. By your grace, turn any fascination with the wrong crowd into a holy zeal for loving and obeying you. Amen.

DAVE AND HEATHER KOPP

AS YOU PRAY TODAY:

- Acknowledge that God's Word is clear on the dangers of associating with the wrong crowd (Proverbs 24:1).
- Pray for boldness for your children to stay away from the enticements of bad companions (Proverbs 1:10).
- Thank God for enabling your children to see through the surface appeal of sin as it is portrayed in music, film, and TV (Proverbs 1:10–19).

THE CHURCH REFORMED

"I will make breath enter you, and you will come to life," says the Lord.

EZEKIEL 37:5

God is in the business of breathing new life into dry bones. There is a great Reformation teaching that the Church reformed is always reforming. I believe this is indeed possible, and steady prayer needs to arise for those called into the ministry of reforming the Church and the churches. We want to rejoice in every new burst of life, every creative force of renewal. We must pray for God to make a way where there is no way.

RICHARD FOSTER

AS YOU PRAY TODAY:

- Intercede for God to provide a clear vision to church leaders to create new solutions for old problems.
- Seek God's renewal in his Church through an outpouring of faithfulness to God's call on individual lives.
- Pray that the witness of a changing, reforming, revitalized Church will touch the hearts of the unsaved.

HOME-SCHOOL STATS

"Fix these words of mine in your hearts and minds. . . . Teach them to your children," says the Lord.

DEUTERONOMY 11:18–19

Home-school students outnumber public school students in 16 states. According to *Home Education: Is It Working?* studies indicate that pupils taught individually achieve 30 percent higher scores on standard achievement tests than their conventional classroom counterparts who are taught in a room of 25 or more. Historical evidence bears this out, too, for prior to the introduction of compulsory school attendance laws, Americans were the most literate people in the world. Sadly, that statistic is no longer true.

S.M.H.

AS YOU PRAY TODAY:

- Place the needs of home-schooled children at the forefront of your prayers.
- Ask God to give parents wisdom and understanding as they teach the lessons of textbooks and godliness.
- Remember the work of organizations that bring home schoolers together for social activities.

MADE IN JAPAN

Manasseh got rid of the foreign gods. Then he restored the altar of the L*ORD and sacrificed fellowship offerings and thank offerings on it.*

2 CHRONICLES 33:15–16

Because the Japanese have very strong ties to their cultural past and to their family values, only those things that have originated in Japan are important to them. School children visit Shinto shrines and learn about emperor worship because these things are part of Japanese culture. These ancient ties hold many Japanese back from becoming Christians. They feel that they would be turning against their culture and their family to accept the Gospel. As a result, some Japanese have blended Christianity with Shintoism to keep peace in the family.

AS YOU PRAY TODAY:

- Ask God to strengthen Japanese Christians to stand firm in their faith against the pressures of family and culture.
- Pray that God will bring the emperor of Japan to Christ.
- Intercede for increased religious freedom so that the Japanese are not forced to believe in Shintoism.

JUDGE AND JUSTIFIER

There is now no condemnation for those who are in Christ Jesus, because through Christ Jesus the law of the Spirit of life set me free from the law of sin and death.

ROMANS 8:1–2

The justification that comes from God himself must be beyond question. If the Judge acquits me, who can condemn me? With this justification we can answer all the roaring and railing of Satan and ungodly men. With this we shall be able to die: with this we shall bodily rise again and face the last judgment. The Lord can blot out all your sins. The Lord is a great forgiver. "I believe in the forgiveness of sins." Do you?

CHARLES H. SPURGEON

AS YOU PRAY TODAY:

- Thank God for the gift of justification that makes you holy in his sight.
- Recognize that this justification extends to every sin from petty misdemeanors to heinous crimes.
- Claim God's forgiveness and ask him to blot out all your sins.

A TALE OF TWO SEAS

Having all that you need, you will abound in every good work.

2 CORINTHIANS 9:8

The Jordan River connects the two seas of Palestine. The Sea of Galilee to the north is vital and alive. Water is constantly flowing in and out. Fishermen still ply its waters.

At the southern end of the Jordan is the Dead Sea. The water in the Dead Sea is so tainted nothing can live in it. The Jordan flows into the Dead Sea, but the Dead Sea has no outlet.

Which sea are you? We're all on the receiving end of God's gifts. Are we on the giving end, too?

S.M.H.

AS YOU PRAY TODAY:

- Thank God for the provisions and gifts he has given you.
- Seek his wisdom for ways to be more like the Sea of Galilee—giving as much as you receive from his hand of blessing.

THE ARK OF GOD

By faith Noah . . . built an ark to save his family.

HEBREWS 11:7

The command given to Noah for his own safety and that of his household I now ask as a question for each father and mother: "Are your children in the ark of God?" You may scoff at it, but it is a very important question. I believe my children have fifty temptations where I had one; and I don't believe it is our business to spend our time in accumulating bonds and stocks. Have I done all to get my children in? That is the question.

DWIGHT L. MOODY

AS YOU PRAY TODAY:

- Are all of your children, grandchildren, nieces and nephews in the ark of God? Pray for each one.
- Have you done all you can to get them in? Ask God to show you.
- Are you living a trustworthy life so that your children will believe your witness to the Gospel?

ABORTION ALTERNATIVES

Before I was born the LORD called me.

ISAIAH 49:1

More than a million legal abortions are performed in the United States every year. Yet more horrifying than the statistics are the reasons many young women give for having abortions: "Having a baby is inconvenient for me right now." "It's my body; I can do what I want." "If I get pregnant, I'll lose my figure." or "It's cheaper than birth control." These young women need to know that there are alternatives to abortion and that these alternatives can be convenient, inexpensive, and beneficial for them, too.

S.M.H.

AS YOU PRAY TODAY:

- Pray for the crisis pregnancy centers in your area. They need funding and volunteers.
- Pray for young women facing unwanted pregnancies. They need to know that God loves them.
- Pray for your involvement in abortion alternatives. Maybe you could speak to young people about abstinence or volunteer some time at a crisis pregnancy center.

MOVING THE MOVIE MAKERS

I will set before my eyes no vile thing.

PSALM 101:3

Hollywood rates every movie it releases. Lower ratings automatically classify a film as a children's movie. Producers know that if a film is rated "R," box office sales will be better. Because of this, some directors purposely add unnecessary violence or nudity to their films to receive a "higher" rating.

But some film studios are changing. DreamWorks' "Prince of Egypt" was an animated gamble that paid off. Warner Brothers' "My Dog Skip" has received lots of airtime on the airlines, delighting passengers. To move the moviemakers into making more family films, we need to support the movies that embrace our values with our pocketbooks.

S.M.H.

AS YOU PRAY TODAY:

- Ask God to give godly vision and values to Hollywood producers, directors, and writers.
- Commit to your own set of godly standards and don't attend a movie that goes beyond it—no matter how popular.

A FLICKERING FLAME

A smoldering wick God will not snuff out. In faithfulness he will bring forth justice.

Isaiah 42:3

The flame of Christianity is flickering in Tunisia. Centuries ago the Christian church was strong in this North African nation, producing leaders like Tertullian and Cyprian. But heresies and the influx of a large Muslim population have reduced the number of evangelical believers in Tunisia to less than 50. Christian leadership is lacking, and the government is yielding to Muslim extremist pressure to rescind religious freedoms. More than half of Tunisian youth support an Islamic state, and many are committed to these extremist groups.

AS YOU PRAY TODAY:

- Intercede for the youth of Tunisia that they will experience a vital Christian witness as they study abroad.
- Pray for the ministry of Christian radio stations reaching out to Tunisians with the Gospel.
- Pray for opportunities for believers to get together and strengthen each other in their faith. Trust needs to be built for this to happen.

A LOVING PROTECTOR

"I will rescue him; I will protect him, for he acknowledges my name," says the Lord.

PSALM 91:14

As part of his oath of office, a president of the United States promises to "preserve, protect, and defend the Constitution of the United States" to the best of his ability. While a mere mortal's ability to perform any task is limited, God's power and ability is limitless. Scripture tells us that "God is love" (1 John 4:8, 16) and that love "always protects" (1 Corinthians 13:7). God's love and protection of us includes the assurance of always. Our God is the God of *always*.

S.M.H.

AS YOU PRAY TODAY:

- Review the promises that God has given about himself in his Word—he always loves, always forgives, always remains the same.
- Remember that God promises to protect each of his children, in good times and in bad.
- Rest in the assurance that God's power is always available for you in unlimited quantities.

A STRONG GRIP

Hezekiah held fast to the LORD
and did not cease to follow him.

2 KINGS 18:6

The nation of Judah was divided. While some people faithfully served God, the majority followed the idolatrous practices of their pagan neighbors. In spite of the prevailing popular opinion, King Hezekiah "held fast to the LORD." In fact, Hezekiah held fast throughout his reign —whether facing an enemy's siege or rejoicing in times of peace.

We should hold fast to the Lord, too, so that our grip won't slip and leave us groping in thin air for help. Holding fast to God will help us outlast the tough times and stand firm in the easy times.

S.M.H.

AS YOU PRAY TODAY:

- Ask God to strengthen your grip by holding you closer to his heart.
- Pray for strength to hold fast in the good times as well as tough ones.
- Faithfully praise God for believers who model a close, committed walk with God.

COURAGE IN CHANGE

I the LORD do not change.

MALACHI 3:6

Change is inevitable—for us, our friends, and family. Feelings crowd in on us whenever we face major changes. When a family member dies, a hole forms in our hearts that never seems to close. Cross-country moves can sever ties with people you thought would be bosom friends for life. Career changes bring new working situations and friendships. Change can be frightening, but God never changes. Knowing this, we can face life's changes willingly, joyfully, and expectantly.

S.M.H.

AS YOU PRAY TODAY:

- Pray for family members dealing with the changes that come from death or divorce.
- Ask God to minister to friends dealing with the change of career and long distance moves.
- Pray that God will wipe away their anxiety and replace it with anticipation, knowing that he is preparing the way for them.

REVIVE US AGAIN

The LORD will again delight in you and make you prosperous, . . . if you obey the LORD your God . . . and turn to the LORD your God with all your heart and with all your soul.

DEUTERONOMY 30:9–10

Wesley L. Duewel recounts that in 1904, when God sent tremendous revival to Wales, a Welsh missionary to India wrote home, begging the people to pray that God would send revival to India. A large group of coal miners began to meet daily at the entrance to the mine for a half-hour before dawn, agreeing in prayer for revival in India. After some weeks of prayer, they received the message, "Revival has come to India."

God's fire of revival is still available! But we must pray—and pray without ceasing until that revival comes.

AS YOU PRAY TODAY:

- Seek God's anointing as you pray for revival in your church and community.
- Ask God to send his Holy Spirit into your life, filling you with contagious joy and enthusiasm.

THE DRUG CONNECTION

Drunkards and gluttons become poor, and drowsiness clothes them in rags.

PROVERBS 23:21

While unemployment problems and getting along with parents troubled teens in the early 1980s, today's teenagers claim that substance abuse is now the biggest problem they face. In fact, almost two-thirds of people age 25 and younger have tried illegal drugs, with the largest percentages found among the affluent and the poor rather than middle income families. In addition, alcohol and drug abuse cost Americans over $200 billion annually in reduced productivity, crime, and related health costs.

S.M.H.

AS YOU PRAY TODAY:

- Remember the victims of substance abuse: babies born addicted, families torn apart, thousands killed in drug-related accidents.
- Pray that God will give children the courage to refuse mind-altering substances despite increasing personal problems.
- Pray for the youth in your church, knowing that regular church attendance reduces drug abuse incidences dramatically.

BOLDNESS IN BARREN MOROCCO

This gospel of the kingdom will be preached in the whole world.

MATTHEW 24:14

Morocco, in the northwest corner of Africa, was once a stronghold of Christianity. Invading Arab armies brought Islam to this barren land and subsequently blotted out the church. Though the country is in desperate need of a change, both economically and religiously, the government refuses to recognize the legality of a Christian church in Morocco. Missionary work is no longer permitted, though foreign Christian workers remain in various secular professions. Persecution of Moroccan believers has been on the increase. In such a hostile environment, bold Christian witness costs believers their families, jobs, and freedom.

AS YOU PRAY TODAY:

- Intercede for Morocco—barren in land, economy, and the hearing of God's Word.
- Pray for boldness for Morocco's few remaining evangelicals.
- Ask God to touch Morocco's leaders to grant religious freedom and legal recognition to Christians so that many more may be saved.

A POPULAR MISCONCEPTION

God determines the number of the stars and calls them each by name.

PSALM 147: 4

The person who falls into the error of thinking of God as nothing more than the Great Architect of the Universe—One who is far removed from the poor human concerns of life—inevitably fails to realize God's personal grace and care. Life for him may develop a sense of duty, but he never comes to regard himself as a son of God, the child of his love. What an eternal loss is his!

J. STUART HOLDEN

AS YOU PRAY TODAY:

- Pray for a balanced spirit that remembers God as the one who made the heavens, but also looks to him to heal hurts.
- Pray for forgiveness for regarding your friendship with the Almighty too lightly.
- Gratefully yield your strength to his service, in any way he calls you.

AWAITING HIS WORKING

We wait in hope for the LORD; he is our help and our shield. In him our hearts rejoice, for we trust in his holy name.

PSALM 33:20–21

How many hours do you spend waiting for something? Maybe for a traffic light or for a person to pick up their telephone. Maybe for an approval for a mortgage or for the birth of a child. Is there any purpose to all of this waiting, anyway?

Yes! While we wait, God puts the pieces of our life's puzzle into place so that his ultimate desire for us will be fulfilled. Our waiting allows for his working. That's what we're waiting for—for God's work to be completed in our lives.

S.M.H.

AS YOU PRAY TODAY:

- Thank God for his control over all of the minutes of your day.
- Commit your waiting moments to him. Relinquish your impatience and anxiety, accepting his peace.
- Use your waiting moments as prayer nuggets: praise the Lord, thank him for a friend, bring a worry to his throne.

THE BLESSING OF MARRIAGE

Marriage should be honored by all.

HEBREWS 13:4

If you can look upon your wife as though she were the only woman in the world and there were none besides; if you can look upon your husband as though he was the only man in the world and there were none besides, then no king, and not even the sun, will shine brighter and clearer in your eyes that your wife and your husband. Would to God that every man might go through life with such a mind.

MARTIN LUTHER

AS YOU PRAY TODAY:

- If you are married, praise God for your spouse, for he or she is God's gift to you.
- If you are single, pray for a married sibling or friend, that they will view their spouse as God's gift.
- Renew your commitment to value marriage as God does—an estate appointed and ordained by him.

WHY NOT?

The righteous will flourish like a palm tree, they will grow like a cedar of Lebanon; planted in the house of the LORD, they will flourish in the courts of our God. They will still bear fruit in old age, they will stay fresh and green.

PSALM 92:12–14

On his eighty-fourth birthday, Dr. Robert G. Lee, pastor emeritus of the First Baptist Church in Memphis, TN, was approached by a friend who asked if he would keep on preaching despite his advanced age. Replied Dr. Lee, "Why not? I am physically able, mentally sound, spiritually desirous and in love with Jesus. Why not keep on preaching as I have done for sixty-two years?"

AS YOU PRAY TODAY:

- Remember those pastors and evangelists who travel and preach the Gospel. Pray for safety and health.
- Rejoice in their dedication and commitment to sharing the good news of Christ.
- Pray that God will raise up godly preachers to carry on the work of older evangelists like Dr. Lee and Dr. Billy Graham.

WIELDING A WORLDLY SWORD

[A ruler] is God's servant to do you good.

ROMANS 13:4

The worldly sword must be merciless for mercy's sake and exercise severity out of sheer goodness. That rogues and rascals are thus punished is not only done in order that the wicked may be punished and the desire for their blood satisfied, but that the good may be defended, and peace and security maintained. These are without doubt Christian works of great mercy, love, and goodness.

MARTIN LUTHER

AS YOU PRAY TODAY:

- Remember all who serve in authority in our state and federal penitentiaries—wardens, guards, and instructors—that God will grant safety and wisdom.
- Ask God to send more Christians to these professions so that inmates can be exposed to a godly witness.

BURIED TREASURE IN QATAR

Even the darkness will not be dark to you, Lord; the night will shine like the day, for darkness is as light to you.

Psalm 139:12

Buried deep under the sands of Qatar are vast oil reserves. The oil reserves have brought great wealth to native Qataris, but the strict Sunni Islam practices of the government have left Qataris poor in spirit. Qatari Christians are rare because the government forbids the proselytism of Muslims. Foreigners come to this barren, desert land on the Arabian Gulf to work in the oil fields because of the high wages they can earn. Though subject to many restrictions, foreign Christians may meet informally for worship in their own homes. These few faithful are the first spark of light in the midst of much spiritual darkness.

AS YOU PRAY TODAY:

- Pray that God will bless and expand the small number of Qatari Christians.
- Pray that believers will find creative ways to share their faith.
- Ask God to work in the life of the Emir of Qatar to bring an end to his abuses of power and to grant religious freedom to all.

GOD'S KINDNESS

God's kindness leads you toward repentance.

ROMANS 2:4

God's kindness is wholly good. When his kindness takes root within us, it permeates our actions, beliefs, and motivations. Planted with a root of God's love, and watered by his compassion and kindness, we will blossom into fruitful believers that reflect the goodness that has been cultivated within. What better way to come to repentance than through the fruit of God's love and kindness?

S.M.H.

AS YOU PRAY TODAY:

- Seek God's kindness. Recognize it. Rejoice in it.
- Allow God's kindness to sink into your soul. Breathe it in. Absorb it.
- Review your life and repent of those things that would keep you from a closer walk with God.

THE PRAYER OF THE UNHOLY

Once you were alienated from God . . . because of your evil behavior. But now he has reconciled you by Christ's physical body through death to present you holy in his sight, without blemish and free from accusation.

COLOSSIANS 1:21–22

We should learn to pray even while we are dwelling on evil. Perhaps we are waging an interior battle over anger, or lust, or pride, or greed, or ambition. We need not isolate these things from prayer. Instead talk to God about what is going on inside that we know displeases him. Lift our disobedience into the arms of the Father; he is strong enough to carry the weight. Sin, to be sure, separates us from God, but trying to hide our sin separates us all the more.

RICHARD FOSTER

AS YOU PRAY TODAY:

- Talk to God about what is going on inside your heart. Bring the good and the bad, even if it displeases him.
- Admit your stubbornness and self-centeredness in prayer.
- Seek his mercy to relieve your inner heart struggles.

PASS IT ON

Jacob blessed [his sons], giving each the blessing appropriate to him.

GENESIS 49:28

In Jacob's last moments, he was still concerned with being a good parent and sharing his faith. Jacob's words reminded his children that all of time is in God's hands. There is no need to fear the future. God has already walked there, and nothing can separate us from his love. As Jacob left his sons a legacy of his faith, so may we pass on to our children God's truth to guide them throughout their lives, too.

S.M.H.

AS YOU PRAY TODAY:

- Resolve to stay on good terms with your children.
- Depend on God's grace to provide times for you to share your faith with your children.
- Pray God's blessings on your children—whether young or grown.

BODY PARTS

You are the body of Christ, and each one of you is a part of it.

1 CORINTHIANS 12:27

Certain parts of the body of Christ are described in detail in 1 Corinthians—the hands, eye, foot. Yet the body parts not mentioned are just as needful to the health of the church. In the same way, God has given you a special gift that is necessary for the health and strength of Christ's body of believers. Can you cook well? That is a gift! Can you sing? That, too, is a gift from God. Don't discount your needfulness just because your gift is not described in detail in the Bible. Your gift may not be mentioned, but it is just as important.

JESSICA RODRIGUEZ, MISSIONARY TO ECUADOR

AS YOU PRAY TODAY:

- Ask God to show you your area of ministry in your church.
- Pray that God will confirm his gift to you.
- Call upon him to show church leaders how best to utilize their congregation's gifts.

NO HOLIDAY

I pray that you may enjoy good health.

3 JOHN 2

At 7:30 p.m. Bob fell and broke his hip. It was Christmas Eve and most stores and restaurants had closed early for the holiday. But when the ambulance crew brought Bob to the hospital emergency room, the lights were on, and the doors were unlocked. Dedicated doctors and nurses relieved his pain while scheduling him for tests and surgery. When Bob finally fell asleep in his hospital room on Christmas afternoon, more dedicated doctors and nurses came to minister to his post-surgical needs, for there's no holiday for hospitals or for the staff who work in them.

S.M.H.

AS YOU PRAY TODAY:

- Thank God for the health care providers you have.
- Pray for God's strength and wisdom for doctors and nurses who work long hours and deal with many patients.
- Ask God's healing touch for those you know who are in the hospital.

TROUBLE IN TURKMENISTAN

It is for freedom that Christ has set us free.

GALATIANS 5:1

The former Soviet republic of Turkmenistan is slowly throwing off its Communist oppression and replacing it with the religion of Islam. Famed for its carpets, oil, and gas production, this Asian land is 80 percent desert. The majority of the nation is poor, so aid from Iran is welcomed. However, with the aid comes the restrictive laws of Islam. Christians are few and many are afraid to witness. Turkmenistan's government faces an uphill battle in legislating democracy, freedom of religion, and economic policy.

AS YOU PRAY TODAY:

- Pray for full freedom of religion so that the Gospel may be spread without hindrance.
- Believers are rare in Turkmenistan. Pray for strength, protection, and increasing numbers.
- Intercede for the government to open its doors to humanitarian efforts by Christian groups. May this be an effective means of sharing the Gospel.

ABSOLUTELY AND FOREVER

If we are faithless, God will remain faithful, for he cannot disown himself.

2 TIMOTHY 2:13

The crowning glory of God is that he never acts out of character. He never falls below his best, he cannot be false to his own blessed nature. If even once you come upon him with no clouds and darkness around him to confuse your mind and tempt you to imaging things that are not there; if even once you meet him face to face, then you know that he always is. You can depend upon that absolutely and forever. What God is, he always is.

ARTHUR JOHN GOSSIP

AS YOU PRAY TODAY:

- Praise God for his faithfulness that always loves, always forgives, always cares.
- Rejoice that God sent his Son to be our visible manifestation of all that God is.
- Pray that as his child you will manifest God's character to others by following the example of Christ.

A FUZZY FOCUS

Who gave man his mouth? Who makes him deaf or mute? Who gives him sight or makes him blind? Is it not I, the LORD?

EXODUS 4:11

Have you ever become so absorbed in your own struggles, your own joys, your own projects, and your own schedules that you begin to wonder how "you" can handle anything else? When we turn our eyes inward this way, our focus gets fuzzy. Our self-sufficiency sets us up for failure. But God can bring clear vision to those eyes blinded by self.

S.M.H.

AS YOU PRAY TODAY:

- Ask God to show you how your struggles can help you grow strong in your faith.
- Recognize that the circumstances that leave you feeling inadequate may be the very thing to teach you dependence on him.
- Pray that God will help you focus on his priorities and plan for your life. Let him be in control.

A BIGGER SHOVEL

"Bring the whole tithe into the storehouse, that there may be food in my house. Test me in this," says the L*ORD* *Almighty, "and see if I will not throw open the floodgates of heaven and pour out so much blessing that you will not have room enough for it."*

MALACHI 3:10

Her daddy was a good churchman, but he didn't tithe. The young girl did. So she told her father about God's challenge in Malachi, and then asked her daddy to try an experiment. "Give God his tithe," she said. "Do it for one month. See what happens." The father agreed; and the young girl prayed. When her daddy sat down at the end of the month to settle the family accounts, a miracle happened. For the first time in their family history there was enough money at the end of the month to pay all of the bills.

S.M.H.

AS YOU PRAY TODAY:

- Prayerfully consider how you give to God. Does your family need to tithe?
- Pray about giving a little extra to cover a special request that you know about. God's storehouse is bigger than yours. Trust him to make up any difference.

ASSOCIATES IN SERVICE

[Paul wrote:] Greet Priscilla and Aquila, my fellow workers in Christ Jesus. They risked their lives for me. Not only I but all the churches of the Gentiles are grateful to them

ROMANS 16:3–4

Into the keeping of God I put
All doings of today. All disappointments, hindrances, forgotten things, negligences. All gladness and beauty, love, delight, achievement.
All that people have done for me, All that I have done for them,
my work and my prayers. And I commit all the people whom I love to his shepherding, to his healing and restoring, to his calling and making;
Through Jesus Christ our Lord.

MARGARET CROPPER

AS YOU PRAY TODAY:

- Pray for those who serve alongside a senior pastor in a church congregation.
- Pray for associates in service in other ministry organizations.
- Ask God to provide balanced priorities, a Christ-focused life, time for prayer, and safety in travel.

MANY HATS

The LORD gives strength to his people;
the LORD blesses his people with peace.

PSALM 29:11

She may be your grocery clerk or hairdresser. He may be your auto mechanic or coworker. After hours they share a similar occupation: they are single parents. Because of many factors, the number of single parents is on the rise in our country. Studies show that children from single parent families are more at risk for scholastic and disciplinary problems, so single parents must wear many hats in their balancing act of being both father and mother. The work is tough, but when done well, the rewards are worth it.

S.M.H.

AS YOU PRAY TODAY:

- Pray for the single parents in your church and neighborhood—for balance between career and family, for a Christ-focused life, and for discernment to sense problems before they arise.
- Ask God to send mentors to single parents to give them practical suggestions for enjoying their parenting years.

QUICKENED IN AFFLICTION

For Christ's sake, I delight in weaknesses, in insults, in hardships, in persecutions, in difficulties. For when I am weak, then I am strong.

2 CORINTHIANS 12:10

Located on the Caspian Sea between Armenia and Turkey, the republic of Azerbaijan broke away from the Soviet Union in 1991. After centuries of domination by other lands, Azeris have begun to transform their government into an Islamic state. Though Azerbaijan officially guarantees freedom of religion, anti-Christian sentiment runs high. Churches have been closed and few Azeri believers feel free to meet publicly. Christian literature can be shared, but distribution is limited since there are so few believers.

AS YOU PRAY TODAY:

- Pray for Azeri believers and the persecution they face. May they be strengthened in affliction.
- Ask God to send workers to distribute Christian literature to this largely unreached nation.
- Pray for the Azeri government to rebuke Islamic extremists and uphold its laws to guarantee freedom of religion to all.

A FAITHFUL GOD

Your faithfulness continues through all generations.

PSALM 119:90

Pastor Bill Hybels tells of a time when he was asked to speak to a large gathering in India. His inexperience and fear of failure had almost immobilized him, but then he made "a faithful God" the object of his attention: "I'm praying to the Creator of the world, the King of the universe, the all-powerful, all-knowing, all-faithful God. I'm praying to the God who has always been faithful to me, who has never let me down no matter how frightened I was or how difficult the situation looked. I am going to trust that he is going to use me tonight. Not because of who I am, but because of who he is. He is faithful."

AS YOU PRAY TODAY:

- Pray a mountain-moving prayer about a problem you are facing, recognizing God's adequacy and faithfulness in all situations.
- Breathe in God's strength and power as you breathe out your fears and anxieties.
- Thank God for the faith he adds to your own when you step out and trust his promises.

LETTING GO

Jesus said, "Whoever loses his life for me will find it."

MATTHEW 16:25

Why does God seemingly require relinquishment before bringing something into being? Frequently we hold on so tightly to the good that we do know that we cannot receive the greater good that we do not know. God has to help us let go of our tiny vision in order to release the greater good he has in store for us. Relinquishment brings to us a priceless treasure: the crucifixion of the will.

RICHARD FOSTER

AS YOU PRAY TODAY:

- Admit your sinful desire to be in control of all of the pieces of your life.
- Confess your fear of what might happen if you give up those areas under your control.
- Let Jesus show you how "Not my will, but yours" can apply to your family, your life, your work.

MRS. GRADY

Follow my example, as I follow the example of Christ.

1 CORINTHIANS 11:1

Helen Grady's gruff manner was actually a façade. She loved children. I eagerly looked forward to my daily visits to her home. She taught me how to get eggs out of the chicken coop without getting pecked, how to light a fire in an old iron stove, and countless other practicalities. She confronted the awful monsters of my childhood dreams, [ending] our dialogues by saying, "Now, honey, let's talk to the Lord." I can still relive, even now, the sense of God's presence. These moments captured my attention, affections, and faith.

JAMES MELVIN WASHINGTON

AS YOU PRAY TODAY:

- Has the Lord been directing you to mentor a younger person? Ask God to help you see what's holding you back.
- Pray that God will send mentors to each child who is important in your life.
- Ask God to search your heart. Can you make Paul's words in 1 Corinthians 11:1 your own?

TAKING SIDES

Count yourselves dead to sin but alive to God.

ROMANS 6:11

Sin in the flesh, inherent in the old nature, is not destroyed when one is born again. That old sin-principle remains in the believer. What takes place at new birth is that a new and divine nature is communicated. Now the old nature has no claim upon me. If it asserts itself, I am to take sides with God against it. Instead of yielding to it, I am to yield myself unto God as one alive from the dead.

HENRY A. IRONSIDE

AS YOU PRAY TODAY:

- Pray for new believers in your church that they will stand firm in their faith and not be discouraged by their struggles.
- Ask God to help you walk after the leading of the Spirit as a mentor for a new believer.
- Thank Christ for his death on the cross for you.

COUNT YOUR BLESSINGS

God will bless us, and all the ends of the earth will fear him.

Psalm 67:7

Did you ever stop to think of the everyday people who are God's blessings in our lives? The paperboy and garbage man bless our lives with their services. The neighborhood mail carrier, supermarket cashier, and bus driver bless our lives, too, by the faithful performance of their duties. Police officers, firefighters, doctors, and nurses all play special roles in our lives. They make our lives run more smoothly. They help to keep us safe and well. Yet too often we overlook these blessings and take them for granted. Let's be a blessing to those who bless our lives by giving thanks for them today.

Conover Swofford

AS YOU PRAY TODAY:

- Inwardly thank God for all those you meet in your daily routine today.
- Invoke God's blessing on their lives.
- Pray for their safety as they do their jobs.

A BALTIC BEACON

Return to the LORD your God,
for he is gracious and compassionate,
slow to anger and abounding in love.
JOEL 2:13

Independent from the Soviet Union since 1991, years of living under Communist oppression have left a devastating moral, economic, and social impact on Latvia. Communist repression of religion was stronger in Latvia than in the other Baltic republics because of a large number of resettled Russian soldiers and factory workers. Missionaries are slowly returning, bringing a literature crusade to unreached parts of the country, an outreach to youth, and leadership training for pastors so that Latvia can become a beacon of hope to others in the Baltic.

AS YOU PRAY TODAY:

- Pray that many will sense their need for God and respond to the Gospel call.
- Ask God's guidance for the government to balance national pride with an influx of ethnic minorities. May there be justice for all.
- Pray for harmony among Latvian believers so that their witness is strengthened and lives are touched.

LOVE'S SHADOW

I, the L*ORD your God, am a jealous God.*
EXODUS 20:5

Love is as strong as death,
its jealousy unyielding as the grave.
SONG OF SONGS 8:6

The Bible, which knows our human hearts, assures us of the jealousy of God. For jealousy is the shadow cast by love. An indifferent wife cannot be jealous; she only becomes jealous when she loves. A jealous God can never be indifferent. He loves with a love so burning and intense that he is passionately jealous for his people. The jealousy of God is also the key to the coming of the Savior. It tells of a love so deep and strong that it will go to any length to sacrifice—even to the giving of the Son of God.

GEORGE H. MORRISON

AS YOU PRAY TODAY:

- Make sure that God is the only One who has full control of your heart.
- Remember that you are the apple of God's eye (Zechariah 2:8).
- Search your heart for unrighteous jealousies that cause division between you and others.

TRUSTWORTHY, TOO

Whoever can be trusted with very little can also be trusted with much.

LUKE 16:10

Grandpa urged Cecie to come out into the lake. The water was wonderful, he said. He promised to hold her hand, too. Slowly, Cecie held out a trembling hand. She felt his firm grip, and together they explored the water with joyous abandon.

The little things in life—keeping our promises, telling the truth—are truly important. Through faithfulness in small things you will please God and gain the sweet trust of those you love.

S.M.H.

AS YOU PRAY TODAY:

- Commit your words, thoughts, and actions to the Lord, asking him to help you be trustworthy in everything.
- Repent of the insincere promises and "little white lies" that fall too easily from our lips.
- Ask God to help you follow through on your commitments and develop habits of dependability.

HOMEBUILDING

Unless the LORD builds the house,
its builders labor in vain.

PSALM 127:1

Let the Lord build your house and look after it. Do not interfere with his work. It falls to him, not you, to look after it. Leave him, who is master of the house and runs it, to look after it. If much is needed in a house, do not worry, God is greater. He who fills heaven and earth will surely be able to fill a house, all the more so because he has undertaken to do so and allows the psalmist to praise him for it.

MARTIN LUTHER

AS YOU PRAY TODAY:

- Pray for your family and the home you are building—a home of godly character not just roofs and walls.
- Ask God to relieve the burdens that worry the members of your family and to bless them with abundance.
- Pray that God will keep your family from covetousness—wanting to be more like the "Joneses" than like Jesus.

A SECOND CHANCE

The word of the LORD came to Jonah a second time.

JONAH 3:1

The Lord called Jonah to deliver a message of repentance to Nineveh, but Jonah didn't answer his call. In fact, Jonah ran away. But the Bible tells us that the Lord called again. This time, after a ride in a fish's belly, Jonah cooperated. He followed God's call, and Nineveh repented. God gave Jonah a second chance that ultimately saved a city. Is there someone in your church who deserves a second chance? A second chance may be just what's needed to follow God's plan, rescue a relationship, or even make a new friend.

S.M.H.

AS YOU PRAY TODAY:

- Ask God:
- Do I need to give someone in your church a second chance at friendship?
- Is God calling me a second time to do something for him?
- Do I have a second chance to repair a broken relationship? What's stopping me?

OUR FATHER'S WORLD

Rejoice in the LORD your God,
for he has given you
the autumn rains in righteousness.
He sends you abundant showers,
both autumn and spring rains, as before.
JOEL 2:23

Do you not think that if the birds and animals could speak, when they see worldly government among men, they would say: "O great and noble men: You enjoy secure possession of life and land, while we are not safe from each other in respect of life or home or food, not even for an hour. Woe to your ingratitude, that you do not see what glorious life our God has given you compared with us beasts."

MARTIN LUTHER

AS YOU PRAY TODAY:

- Thank God for the provisions of home and food that you have, and for the animals that inhabit that life with you.
- Consider the policies pending in our government for land conservation and environmental concerns.
- Reflect on ways you can be a better steward of our Father's world.

SPIRITUAL HUNGER IN THE HIMALAYAS

All the ends of the earth
have seen the salvation of our God.

PSALM 98:3

Bhutan is a small kingdom in the eastern Himalayas. Though this Buddhist state forbids public worship or evangelism by any other religion, missionaries have ministered in Bhutan in medical and aid settings. Some Bhutanese have become Christians because of the witness of Indian believers visiting and working in Bhutan. But Bhutanese Christians are routinely arrested, imprisoned, and tortured.

AS YOU PRAY TODAY:

- Intercede for the work of Bible translation in the Dzongkha language that God will raise up new translators to replace those who have had to leave the country.
- Pray for the opening of Bhutan to the free spread of the Gospel message.
- Ask God to help the silent witness of missionaries and believers to reach the hearts of the spiritually hungry in Bhutan.

HIS POWERFUL HAND

"With my great power and outstretched arm I made the earth and its people," says the Lord.

JEREMIAH 27:5

God's awesome power is available to us through the simple words of prayer. Our prayers may be petitions of need or affirmations of great faith. English Archbishop William Temple prayed a blessing over his congregation:

May the love of the Lord Jesus draw us to himself;
May the power of the Lord Jesus strengthen us in his service;
May the joy of the Lord Jesus fill our souls.
May the blessing of God almighty,
the Father, the Son, and the Holy Ghost,
be amongst you
and remain with you always.

AS YOU PRAY TODAY:

- Praise God for his awesome power.
- Thank God for his promise to use his power for the benefit of his children.
- Ask God for his power to strengthen you to do his will today.

A PEACEFUL SOUL

I will listen to what God the LORD will say;
he promises peace to his people, his saints.

PSALM 85:8

In his *Benediction for a Peaceful Soul,* Anthony Binga, Jr. prays: "May the Lord save you from any painful regrets when the reaping time shall come. But may you all have so lived, that no arrow from God's quiver of justice can pierce your soul, nor mountain of guilt sink you down.

"But may you all find your portion, with the redeemed and sanctified out of every nation, tongue and people, around the burnished throne of God, with everlasting shouts of joy and praise upon your lips. Amen."

AS YOU PRAY TODAY:

- Seek God's gift of peace in your innermost being. Feel his presence strip away all of your cares.
- Center your thoughts on God's great love for you. Sense his Spirit filling you with his grace.
- Rejoice in the realized freedom of living in God's peace.

"PLAN A"

Esther sent this reply to Mordecai: "Go, gather together all the Jews who are in Susa, and fast for me. . . . I and my maids will fast as you do. When this is done, I will go to the king, even though it is against the law. And if I perish, I perish."

ESTHER 4:15–16

God has a plan for your family, a way he wants things to be. His "Plan A" may mean some difficult choices, some fearsome paths, some uncertain outcomes. But your family has a choice, and they may choose to follow the crowd instead of the Creator.

Esther had a choice, too. She could have chosen to stand aside and let someone else be Israel's spokesperson. But because of her faith, Esther chose God's "Plan A." What choice will your family make?

S.M.H.

AS YOU PRAY TODAY:

- Acknowledge God's graciousness in offering your family a choice to follow after his will.
- Pray that God will guide your family to make the choices that will honor him, choices that will reflect his "Plan A" for their lives.

PRACTICING PREACHERS

Imitate those who through faith and patience inherit what has been promised.

HEBREWS 6:12

Role models are people you respect for setting worthy examples. Mentors are people who've taken role modeling to the next level by teaching you the details of who they are, how they think, what they've done and why they have something worth pursuing. Without congruency between creeds and deeds, there is hypocrisy and no credibility. Mentors earn respect through a lifetime of "practicing what they preach."

DICK BIGGS

AS YOU PRAY TODAY:

- Intercede for God to send marriage mentors to struggling young couples in your church.
- Ask God to provide financial mentors to believers drowning in debt.
- Search your heart and ask God to help you find a mentor for that area of your life that is lacking—no matter how big or small.

GAMBLING WITH OUR GRANDPARENTS

Even when I am old and gray, do not forsake me, O God.

PSALM 71:18

A gray-haired woman struggled onto a crowded bus heading to Canada. She wasn't going to gamble at the casinos like the rest of the passengers. She was going to buy prescription drugs. Though her prescribed medication was available in the United States, Medicare required a less expensive substitute be dispensed. However, the substitute made the woman ill. Her prescription medicine was available in Canada for a lower price. So the woman made the 10-hour, round-trip bus ride every month to buy medication that is readily available in the United States for employed persons, but unavailable to our senior citizens.

S.M.H.

AS YOU PRAY TODAY:

- Pray for wisdom as leaders review medical policies for senior citizens. We're gambling with our grandparents' health, and policies need to change.
- Ask God to show you how your church can help senior citizens obtain the medical care they need.

OMAN'S NEW DAWN

The path of the righteous is like the first gleam of dawn, shining ever brighter till the full light of day.

PROVERBS 4:18

With advancing oil sales and a steadily increasing economy, the Sultan of Oman has promised his people a new dawn of prosperity. But the nation of Oman struggles under the darkness of Islam, too. Though churches for foreigners are permitted, there are no Omani churches, and Omani Christians number less than 20. A strong missionary presence is still felt in the medical community and in a Bible society and bookshops that distribute Christian Arabic literature. Christian radio broadcasts are also becoming popular, and some have come to the Lord as a result.

AS YOU PRAY TODAY:

- Pray that foreign Christians will live exemplary lives of witness for their Omani neighbors.
- Ask God to strengthen and protect Omani believers and help them give bold witness for Christ.
- Pray that the government will guarantee political freedom to plant Omani churches.

A STRONG DELIVERER

You are my hiding place, O Lord;
you will protect me from trouble
and surround me with songs of deliverance.
PSALM 32:7

Hezekiah's people faced sure destruction from Sennacherib's army. A general came to Hezekiah with a letter from Sennacherib that insulted God and demanded Jerusalem's immediate surrender. Soldiers taunted Jerusalem's inhabitants, intimidating them with tales of their impending doom. Yet Hezekiah's first response to an overwhelming enemy wasn't fear or verbal combat. Hezekiah prayed. He called for God's mighty hand of deliverance. When we face an overwhelming enemy, may we follow Hezekiah's example, sidestep fear, and immediately carry our needs to our strong Deliverer instead

S.M.H.

AS YOU PRAY TODAY:

- Thank God for the many times that he has delivered you in small things.
- Rejoice in God's power and strength to deliver you from your overwhelming enemies.
- Ask God to remind you to come to him first when everything around you looks impossible.

A POWERFUL COMMAND

Cast all your anxiety on God because he cares for you.

1 PETER 5:7

Some people go reeling and staggering all through life. They put on a whining voice and tell you what "a hard time they have had." Sometimes they go into their closet and close their door, and they get so carried away and lifted up that they forget their trouble; but they just take it up again the moment they get off their knees. Leave your sorrow now; cast all your care upon him. Christ says, "Come unto me." With the command comes the power.

DWIGHT L. MOODY

AS YOU PRAY TODAY:

- Bring your worries to the Lord and leave the whole bundle at his feet.
- Thank God for the promise of his care and his willingness to bear your burdens.
- Rejoice and let your face reflect it, knowing that God is taking care of everything in his time and his way.

A QUIET CHAT

The LORD makes me lie down in green pastures,
he leads me beside quiet waters,
he restores my soul.
PSALM 23:2–3

Have you ever tried to pray when you have a "zillion" things happening around you? Praying in such situations is not easy. For that matter, trying to do anything that requires concentration is difficult when chaos surrounds you. Your friends are no different. They need time, too, away from life's distractions to have a quiet chat with their heavenly Father. Can you help them find that quiet time?

JESSICA RODRIGUEZ, MISSIONARY TO ECUADOR

AS YOU PRAY TODAY:

- Pray that God will give you clarity of thought and purpose as you pray for your friends today.
- Ask God to give your friends a chance today to have a quiet chat with him.
- Gain God's feedback on ways that you might be able to help your friends find that quiet time. Can you help them get a project completed? Babysit a child? Volunteer to run an errand?

THE WITNESS OF THE CHURCH

In the church God has appointed first of all apostles, second prophets, third teachers, then workers of miracles, also those having gifts of healing, those able to help others, those with gifts of administration, and those speaking in different kinds of tongues.

1 CORINTHIANS 12:28

The first work of the church is seeking and saving the lost; its second work is feeding the flock; and its third work is training the membership for intelligent service. If the institutions connected with the church are allowed to put any one of these three things in the background, they do more harm than good. In contrast, if the institutions are carried on in the spirit of prayer and never lose sight of for a moment the intention of winning men for Christ, they may be very helpful.

R. A. TORREY

AS YOU PRAY TODAY:

- Is your church working to save the lost? Ask God what more can be done.
- Is your church caring for other believers? Ask God what more you could do.
- Is your church training its members for service? Ask God what more you all could do.

AT ODDS

Wash away all my iniquity
and cleanse me from my sin, O Lord.
For I know my transgressions,
and my sin is always before me.
PSALM 51:2–3

He owns his own business, serves on several church committees, and enjoys his vacations with his wife and children on a lake not far from home, but he is also addicted to pornographic videos. She teaches in a Christian high school and volunteers at a local hospital, but the trunk of her car is littered with pornographic magazines.

Pornography is available in airport newsstands and neighborhood grocery stores. And its message puts hearts at odds with the Creator as it feeds the sinful desires of sexual fantasy that the Bible calls "lust."

S.M.H.

AS YOU PRAY TODAY:

- Ask God to give local authorities boldness to enforce laws prohibiting the sale of pornography.
- Intercede for deliverance for Christian brothers and sisters addicted to pornography.
- Seek God's protection for those you love from the enticements of pornographic "entertainment."

UNITED IN CHRIST

"Return to me, and I will return to you," says the LORD Almighty.

MALACHI 3:7

Britain needs prayer. Increasing violence, divorce, suicide, and political ineffectiveness have brought about widespread dissatisfaction. In this land of Calvin and Wesley, Christians are complacent in the face of moral collapse. Many young people in the United Kingdom have no contact with or knowledge of Christianity. Cathedrals are little more than museums to a dead and dying belief system. New Age beliefs, Eastern mysticism, and the influx of non-Christian religions have eroded the Christian foundation of this monarchy. The United Kingdom needs to be united again in Christ.

AS YOU PRAY TODAY:

- Pray for Britain's return to the godly heritage of its past. Revival is needed.
- Ask God to stir lethargic Christians to reach out to young people seeking spiritual answers.
- Thank God that the eroding social fabric has caused some to reconsider yielding to the Savior.

GOD'S CURE

My comfort in my suffering is this:
Your promise preserves my life, O Lord.

Psalm 119:50

God's soul and nature are the blood of the universe. Medicine is merely a coaxer. Its business is to say to the part affected, "Wake up and get well." If a man gets well, he cures himself—often, thanks to the doctor; more often, thanks to the nurse. Yet it is the heart of God that carries restoration, inspiration, aspiration, and final victory. As long as God is "the Father of compassion and the God of all comfort," this world will not go to rack and ruin.

Henry Ward Beecher

AS YOU PRAY TODAY:

- Bring your illness, heartache, and sorrow to God. He knows how to heal them all.
- Know that whatever comes your way, God will use it for good.
- Ask God to show you someone who needs to share the comfort you have already received.

SECRET IDOLS

Teach me your way, O LORD,
and I will walk in your truth;
give me an undivided heart,
that I may fear your name.
PSALM 86:11

When the Israelites took over Canaan, they kept up the pretense of their worship of God, but also secretly followed the idolatrous customs of their neighbors. Their actions weren't secret from God, however. He knows everything!

How like those ancient Israelites we are. We often blend our worship of God with the idols of our culture. How often have we trusted credit cards to provide for our needs? Do we worship at secret altars of power and success throughout the week, and give God only a few hours on the weekend?

S.M.H.

AS YOU PRAY TODAY:

- Ask God to illumine any secret idols in your life.
- Claim God's forgiveness for following the idolatrous ways of our culture.
- Ask God to give you a holy attitude toward your possessions, job, money, power, success, etc. Use them all for his glory.

FACING LIONS

Your enemy the devil prowls around like a roaring lion looking for someone to devour. Resist him, standing firm in the faith. . . . And the God of all grace, . . . will himself restore you and make you strong, firm and steadfast.

1 PETER 5:8–10

A lion is coming toward you. Your natural instinct is to flee in fear. But if you run, the lion will immediately chase you. Your only recourse is to "stand firm."

The Bible says that the devil is "a roaring lion," and we must oppose him by "standing firm in the faith" (1 Peter 5:8–9). Yet we don't have to stand in fear. The Bible promises that even though the lion (the devil) may stalk your family, you can stand, without fear, and face him, for God has promised that the devil "will flee from you" (James 4:7).

JESSICA RODRIGUEZ

AS YOU PRAY TODAY:

- Ask God to open your eyes to the lions facing your family.
- Pray that your family, when faced with their own personal "lions," will not fear, but trust God's promises.

THE WORDS OF GOD'S WORD

We . . . thank God continually because, when you received the word of God, . . . you accepted it not as the word of men, but as it actually is, the word of God, which is at work in you who believe.

1 THESSALONIANS 2:13

It takes thirty syllables in the Kaiwá language of Brazil to say, "The lame walk; the blind see." Final revision and proofing of the Ndogo New Testament is finished but distribution is threatened because of unrest in the area. The Pitjantjatjara and Warlpiri of Australia will receive the Bible in their languages soon. These are some of the exciting reports from Bible translators worldwide. These missionaries must continue their work because there are still millions who have never read the Bible in their own language.

S.M.H.

AS YOU PRAY TODAY:

- Pray for members of translation teams and their families for this is a long-term commitment that often means long periods of separation.
- Ask God to raise up many long-term volunteers to work as support staff.
- Pray for Bible translation teams that have had to relocate because of war and civil strife.

A VIOLENT TIE

Discretion will protect you,
and understanding will guard you.
Wisdom will save you from the ways of wicked men,
from men whose words are perverse.
PROVERBS 2:11–12

When pornography increases, so does violent crime. Rape rates are highest in states that have high sales of sexually explicit materials. Rapists are fifteen times more likely than non-offenders to have had exposure to hard-core pornography before the age of ten. Following a crackdown in Cincinnati, OH on adult bookstores, X-rated movie theaters, and massage parlors, there was a 42 percent decrease in prostitution, assaults, and drug trafficking, and an 83 percent decrease in rapes, robberies, and aggravated assaults.

S.M.H.

AS YOU PRAY TODAY:

- Pray that God will give law enforcement wisdom and safety as they deal with violent crime.
- Pray that sales of sexually explicit materials will halt and that laws that are on the books will be enforced.
- Pray for God's protection for your neighborhood.

THE LAND OF PAUL AND SILAS

Paul chose Silas and left, commended by the brothers to the grace of the Lord. He went through Syria and Cilicia, strengthening the churches.

ACTS 15:40–41

The city of Antioch in Syria first heard the Gospel message from Paul and Silas (Acts 15). In the centuries following that life-changing visit, Syrian Christians have been a respected minority in their largely Muslim land. Yet Syrian law allows authorities to hold persons suspected of threatening the government without legal safeguards. This has led to harassment of Christians who try to share their faith. Missionaries are denied visas, so believers can only witness in informal settings at home or at work.

AS YOU PRAY TODAY:

- Pray that believers will recapture the zeal of the first Christians in Antioch.
- Ask God to continue the growth of churches and fellowship groups despite government restrictions and pressure.
- Pray that the government of Syria will become increasingly tolerant to other faiths. Pray for the salvation of the Syrian president.

THE LIVING GOD

You will know that the living God is among you.

JOSHUA 3:10

The Israelites were camped outside of Canaan when Joshua assured the people of God's presence and of God's promise to help them. As a token of this presence and promise, Joshua reminded the people that their trust was in a "living God," a God of power, not one of the dead gods of the Canaanites. Though they could not see God or did not carry an image of him as the Canaanites did, the living God would be among them to go with them into the land. What a promise! What a blessing!

S.M.H.

AS YOU PRAY TODAY:

- Give God homage for his power and greatness even though you cannot see or touch him.
- Know that before you face anything today, God has already touched it with his presence.
- Pray for a deeper sense of knowing the living God in all his glory.

GOD'S ABUNDANT BLESSINGS

You crown the year with your bounty, Lord, and your carts overflow with abundance.

Psalm 65:11

Don't overlook the small things. God's blessings are abundant. Be thankful for the purring of a soft kitten, the snoring of a contented dog, the home you have, the friends and family who help fill it, the enjoyable jobs, the days of good health, enough food to eat, and more, safety in travel and in rest, clothes to wear and clothes to wash, furnishings for home and hearth, reliable transportation, for rain that makes things grow, the sun that warms the earth, and God's love that makes it all possible.

S.M.H.

AS YOU PRAY TODAY:

- Make this a day of thanksgiving. In every spare minute find something to be thankful for.
- Leave your petitions and requests aside for one day. Make this a day of praise for God's blessings—both big and small.

UNEQUALLY YOKED

[Jehoram] married a daughter of Ahab. He did evil in the eyes of the LORD.

2 KINGS 8:18

Jehoram had been raised in a godly home. His father, King Jehoshaphat, had ruled Judah in peace because he followed God's ways. But Jehoram made a poor choice in a wife. He married wicked King Ahab's daughter and "did evil in the eyes of the LORD." Though this young man had had a godly father, the influence of his wife turned him against God.

Our children's mates will make a difference to their lives. Whether your children are 6 or 26, they and their spouses-to-be need your prayers.

S.M.H.

AS YOU PRAY TODAY:

- Commit your children and their friends to the Lord.
- Ask God to guard your children's choice of a mate so that they will not be enticed away from him.
- Pray that your children will date and marry only those who truly love and serve Christ.

GOD'S NAVY

Jesus began to teach by the lake. The crowd that gathered around him was so large that he got into a boat and sat in it out on the lake, while all the people were along the shore at the water's edge.

MARK 4:1

Jesus used boats to take him to new places of ministry. Modern-day missionaries are following his example. Ships outfitted with mobile medical bays encircle the globe, bringing aid, discipleship programs, and Christian literature to thousands of isolated communities. Flotillas based in New Zealand reach out to Pacific islanders. Ships on the Amazon River reach remote tribes. And boats plying the waterways of Europe bring the Gospel to fishing ports and vacation spots.

S.M.H.

AS YOU PRAY TODAY:

- Pray for the spiritual health and safety for all members of God's navy.
- Ask God to provide technically qualified crew members, without whom the ships cannot sail.
- Pray that believers will generously fund these strategic ministries as costs rise annually.

DESPERATE LIVES

The Spirit of the Sovereign LORD is on me, because the LORD has anointed me . . . to bestow on them a crown of beauty instead of ashes, the oil of gladness instead of mourning, and a garment of praise instead of a spirit of despair.

ISAIAH 61:1, 3

Recently a student at my school attended his cousin's funeral. His cousin had committed through suicide. We would prefer to forget this issue, but teen suicide is on the increase. Part of the dilemma facing young people is the lack of hope that most teens experience. They feel they have no way to conquer life's difficulties and, in desperation, take their own lives. Our teens do not know Christ and have little influence, or exposure to, those Christians around them. We may feel inept to help these struggling teens, but prayer is a powerful weapon.

MIKE WILSON

AS YOU PRAY TODAY:

- Pray that the Lord encourage a struggling teen.
- Pray for teens that are contemplating suicide to understand the value of their lives.
- Pray for teens in to accept Christ as their Savior.

DEVASTATING ETHNIC DIFFERENCES

Above all, love each other deeply, because love covers over a multitude of sins.

1 PETER 4:8

The breakup of Yugoslavia in 1992 led to the formation of several smaller countries, including Bosnia. However, large-scale land grabs by Serbian and Croatian forces intent on taking Bosnia's land as their own left many Bosnian villages destroyed, their women violated, and children murdered. Hostilities prevail in towns where just a few years earlier different religions and cultures lived peacefully. Bosnian Muslims are also very resistant to the Gospel, believing that Christians—Orthodox Serbs and Catholic Croats—are to blame for their suffering.

AS YOU PRAY TODAY:

- Pray for peace and justice in Bosnia.
- Pray for a strong, effective witness to develop in every major city and village.
- Ask God to convict Bosnian Christians of their hatred and to instead reach out in love to other religions and cultures.

UNDENIABLE SELF-EXISTENCE

God said to Moses, "I AM WHO I AM. This is what you are to say to the Israelites."

EXODUS 3:14

The divine name "I AM" is a declaration of God's eternal and immutable self-existence. He is pure being. Nothing has brought or could bring Him into existence. Nor could anything ever cause Him to cease to be. He has always existed and will always exist because He *is* existence. There is no other attribute of God that better stands as a summation of his nature than this one.

CHARLES R. SWINDOLL

AS YOU PRAY TODAY:

- Who do you believe that God is? Reflect on his eternal self-existence.
- Rejoice that God wants you to know him better, just as he wanted Moses to know him, too.
- God always was, always is, and always will be. Meditate on that and how it affects your joys and concerns.

GOOD GOSSIP

A gossip betrays a confidence,
but a trustworthy man keeps a secret.

PROVERBS 11:13

"Oh, I could never say anything bad about my husband," the professor's wife exclaimed. "That just wouldn't be right." Her comment touched our roomful of young marrieds and brought our whispers to a halt. We knew that her husband had faults; everyone does. Yet she continued brightly, "After all, when one person talks about a second person to a third person, that's gossip. I only want to spread 'good gossip' about my husband, otherwise it could hurt both of us." That day the young marrieds decided to follow her "good gossip" rule, and their marriages have never been happier.

S.M.H.

AS YOU PRAY TODAY:

- Prayerfully consider your conversations with others. Are you prone to gossip?
- Confess your tendency to cover gossip under the guise of prayer requests.
- Ask God to signal you in a way that you will recognize if you slip into a negative, gossip situation.

BLIND SPOTS

Accept one another, then, just as Christ accepted you, in order to bring praise to God.

ROMANS 15:7

At a recent family get-together, Ann briefly glanced around the room as she talked and laughed with her cousins. She noticed that her Aunt Barbara was sitting alone in the corner of the room picking at her dessert and muttering to herself. Aunt Barbara, the second wife of Ann's late Uncle John, was a bit eccentric and had never really fit in with the rest of the family. Some of the cousins secretly called her "Aunt Blah-Blah" because of her habit of talking to herself. At this moment, though, Ann realized that Aunt Barbara was probably talking to herself because no one else would.

AS YOU PRAY TODAY:

- Ask God to bring to mind a family member that needs to know that he or she belongs.
- Ask for God's love for that family member and pray that he will remind you to show special kindness the next time you see him or her.
- Pray a special blessing over that person right now.

DAYCARE PRAYERS

Jesus said, "Whoever welcomes one of these little children in my name welcomes me; and whoever welcomes me does not welcome me but the one who sent me."

MARK 9:37

When daycare or nursery workers care for the small ones in their charge, may this be their daily prayer: "Give me, good Lord, an humble, lowly, quiet, peaceable, patient, charitable, kind and filial and tender mind, every shade, in fact, of charity, with all my words and all my works, and all my thoughts, to have a taste of thy holy blessed Spirit."

THOMAS MORE

AS YOU PRAY TODAY:

- Pray for the babysitters, childcare workers, and nursery staff who minister to our children when we are away.
- Petition God for health, strength, and a compassionate heart for these workers.
- Ask God to give wisdom to those who hire daycare providers, alerting them to those who could be inexperienced or unkind.

MEDICAL ETHICS

My frame was not hidden from you
when I was made in the secret place, Lord.
When I was woven together in the depths of the earth,
your eyes saw my unformed body.
PSALM 139:15–16

We all want to cure Parkinson's disease, juvenile diabetes, and Alzheimer's disease. Stem cell research may hold the key to curing these major illnesses, we are told. But what isn't as loudly publicized is that the cells used for research would come from embryonic cells taken from aborted babies. Does the possibility of curing three major illnesses make this embryonic research ethical?

Medical ethics will take their cue from legislation; are we making sure that legislation takes its cue from God?

AS YOU PRAY TODAY:

- Reflect on your familiarity with medical research and the ethical questions facing Congress. If you don't know what's going on, find out.
- Pray for wisdom for researchers to find ways to cure modern illnesses without trespassing against godly standards.

THE CHURCH IN RUSSIA

The eyes of the Lord are on the righteous
and his ears are attentive to their prayer,
but the face of the Lord is against those who do evil.
1 PETER 3:12

Communist leaders once boasted that within a few years they would parade the last Christian in the USSR on television so that the entire world would see that Christianity was a religion for the elderly and mentally unstable. Concerned Christians throughout the world began to pray for the Soviet Union, asking God to grant complete religious liberty and the free distribution of Bibles. When the Soviet Union collapsed in 1990, these prayers were answered.

AS YOU PRAY TODAY:

- Praise God that he is stronger than human ideologies. His words are not boasts; they are reality.
- Pray for the church in Russia. Years of oppression have left buildings in ruins, millions murdered or imprisoned, and pastors disillusioned.
- Ask God to strengthen Russian Christians who face a national identity full of deceit, fear, and low moral standards.

JEHOVAH SHALOM

The God of peace will be with you.

PHILIPPIANS 4:9

When you mention the word *peace* people visibly relax. The traditional Jewish greeting is *shalom*, meaning "peace"—a wish for completeness and well being that can only come from God. An aspect of God's nature, peace carries with it the ideas of security, contentment, prosperity, and an end to strife. When you immerse yourself in God's peace, it is as if your spirit relaxes in a gently swaying hammock of safety, refreshed by the balmy breezes of tranquility. Have you ever felt this kind of peace? Do you want to experience it more often? Get to know "the God of peace."

S.M.H.

AS YOU PRAY TODAY:

- Rest in Jehovah Shalom—the God of peace. Release your cares and concerns to him.
- Feel your soul made complete and whole, safe in God's hand.
- Acknowledge the touch of God's Spirit on your life as you share his peace with others.

HEARING AND DOING

The seed on good soil stands for those with a noble and good heart, who hear the word, retain it, and by persevering produce a crop.

LUKE 8:15

You are to be "a doer" in your Christianity and not merely a hearer. The Lord wants his servants not only to receive his wages and eat his bread and dwell in his house and belong to his family—but also to do his work. Think not because your doings cannot justify you, or put away one single sin, that therefore it matters not whether you do anything at all. Make your calling and election sure. Be a doing Christian.

J. C. RYLE

AS YOU PRAY TODAY:

- Ask God to stir your heart to show you where you are in your faith and where he wants you to be.
- Ask God to forgive you for doubting his ability to use you to do his will.
- Ask God to show you how you can let your light shine for him every day this week.

SEVENTY-SEVEN TIMES

Be kind and compassionate to one another forgiving each other, just as in Christ God forgave you.

EPHESIANS 4:32

Peter once asked Jesus how many times he should forgive his brother. Jesus replied, "Seventy-seven times" (Matthew 18:22). Jesus' reply was an idiom that signified that we should show each other infinite forgiveness regardless of the number of wrongs we may have suffered. Family and friends are irreplaceable blessings from God, but sometimes they will hurt us by their words or actions. Our attempts to reconcile with them should not stop at some magic number. We should love and forgive and reconcile an infinite seventy-seven times.

S.M.H.

AS YOU PRAY TODAY:

- Recall those friends or family members who have said or done something to hurt you.
- Bring each one to the foot of the cross. Ask God to restore your relationship.
- Seek God's forgiveness for harboring ill feeling toward these people.

SINGLE SIGHT

An unmarried man is concerned about the Lord's affairs. . . . An unmarried woman . . . [is] devoted to the Lord in both body and spirit.

1 CORINTHIANS 7:32, 34

Though some view church singles' activities as a "meat market"—a place to scan the available Christian singles in a church and choose a mate—most singles agree that they attend a church singles group looking for fellowship and a sense of family, a safe, accepting community for growing in the Lord. Singles are not people just biding their time until they get married. Singles are our brothers and sisters in the Lord.

S.M.H.

AS YOU PRAY TODAY:

- Singles face many challenges to their Christian commitment. Pray that God will give strength and respect to them to remain sexually pure.
- Ask God to guide single persons in their choices of career, home, and friends.
- Pray for the single people you know—that they will have strength to persevere in their faith.

GOOD NEIGHBORS

If you really keep the royal law found in Scripture, "Love your neighbor as yourself," you are doing right.

JAMES 2:8

If the family next door put lighted pink flamingos in direct line of your dining room windows or placed a pile of stinky, rotten garbage within easy smell of your favorite hammock, you'd say those folks weren't being good neighbors. In like fashion, whenever states that border each other pass legislation that adversely impacts life across the state line, that's not being good neighbors, either. Pending legislation in neighboring states should concern you, for it might bring something worse to your hometown than lighted pink flamingos.

S.M.H.

AS YOU PRAY TODAY:

- Lift the legislators from neighboring states to God for wisdom and discernment in their decisions.
- Pray that your legislators will follow good neighbor policies as they decide on and enact your state's laws.
- Ask God to give guidance and wisdom to national leaders who help direct state policies.

MAURITANIA

Some sat in darkness and the deepest gloom,
prisoners suffering in iron chains. . . .
Then they cried to the LORD *in their trouble,*
and he saved them from their distress.

PSALM 107:10, 13

Mauritania, in northwestern Africa, is one of the least evangelized nations in the world. More than 99 percent of its people are professing Muslims. Freedom of religion is non-existent. A confession of Christ is legally punishable by death. Maures are forbidden to even enter the homes of foreign Christians. Further complicating the spread of the Gospel is a low literacy rate and lack of Christian material available in local languages.

AS YOU PRAY TODAY:

- Pray for innovative ways to bring the Gospel to this closed land.
- Pray for strength for the few believers in Mauritania, that their witness will burn even brighter.
- Pray that Mauritanian leaders will lower the barriers to the Gospel and Christian humanitarian outreach.

ENERGIZED FAITH

[You] through faith are shielded by God's power until the coming of the salvation that is ready to be revealed in the last time.

1 PETER 1:5

Every truth that we honestly believe in becomes an energy in our life. Every genuine belief is a force. But many of the beliefs we profess to hold are as void of life and power as the dry bones in the valley of the prophet's vision. Some of the primary truths of our Christian faith would come upon us with all the surprise of new revelations if we once really felt their power.

JOHN DANIEL JONES

AS YOU PRAY TODAY:

- Worship the Sovereign King with awe; come into his presence with humble praise.
- Ask God to make the truths of your faith real in your life this week.
- Pray that his power will fill your experiences so unmistakably that you'll know it is his doing.

A PROPER FOCUS

Love the Lord your God with all your heart and with all your soul.

MARK 12:30

Friends or family can give good counsel about some things, but only God can always lead us in the right direction. Only God knows us better than we know ourselves. Following his direction will ultimately give us focus and purpose in life. And when pleasing God is our primary focus, life gets a lot simpler. We find time to fulfill his will by meeting the needs of others. We begin to look for opportunities to love others more. Loving God first provides the focus we need to keep all of life in proper perspective.

S.M.H.

AS YOU PRAY TODAY:

- Confess those times when you have not loved God with your whole heart.
- Ask God's forgiveness for any selfishness that chooses your way instead of his.
- Commit your heart to pursuing his will and sharing his love with others.

GOD'S LAMP

Your word is a lamp to my feet
and a light for my path.
PSALM 119:105

Lord, May my children realize how much they need your refreshment. May my children take risks to build their lives on your Word. May my children take genuine delight in studying the Bible. May my children crave the Bible more than any other book.

I pray, Lord, that by loving your Word, my children will receive important warnings about life and be blessed with great personal reward. Amen.

DAVID & HEATHER KOPP

AS YOU PRAY TODAY:

- Pray that God's Word will be the guide used by your children to make wise decisions.
- Believe that God's Word will be their yardstick to determine their philosophies and lifestyle.
- Rejoice that your children will always revere, honor, and worship the Lord because of their love for his Word.

HUMAN SYMPATHY

Carry each other's burdens, and in this way you will fulfill the law of Christ.

GALATIANS 6:2

There are thousands of families that could easily be reached if we had thousands of Christians going to them and entering into sympathy with their sorrows. That is what they want. This poor world is groaning and sighing for sympathy. I am quite sure it was that in Christ's life that touched the hearts of the common people. He made himself one with them.

DWIGHT L. MOODY

AS YOU PRAY TODAY:

- Pray for an opportunity to reach out to someone and help carry his or her burden.
- Ask God to open your eyes to the ways you could be of service.
- Pray for a soft and compassionate heart that reflects Christ to those around you.

A HOUSE AFIRE

If the watchman sees the sword coming and does not blow the trumpet to warn the people. . . . I will hold the watchman accountable.

EZEKIEL 33:6

Our nation is experiencing a decline in ethics and morals, and a rise in homelessness, poverty, and drug abuse. We have a responsibility to stay informed, involved, and vocal about these crises facing our nation. Corrie ten Boom wrote: "Suppose that your house were afire, and I went calmly about straightening pictures, what would you say? Would you think me merely stupid or very wicked?" Our nation is on fire. As its watchmen, what are we doing to extinguish it?

S.M.H.

AS YOU PRAY TODAY:

- Ask God to raise up godly watchmen to speak out against national injustices.
- Ask God to show you how you can help extinguish the fires of sin in our land.
- Pray that God will have mercy on our country and give us back our God-fearing conscience.

FROM SHAH TO SHIITE

Even though I was once a blasphemer and a persecutor and a violent man, I was shown mercy because I acted in ignorance and unbelief. The grace of our Lord was poured out on me abundantly, along with the faith and love that are in Christ Jesus.

1 Timothy 1:13–14

In 1979, the Shah of Iran was deposed in a violent overthrow by Shiite Muslim extremists. The theocratic tyranny of the Ayatollah Khomeini and his successors has proved more corrupt and cruel than any prior system in Iran. Despite constitutional guarantees of religious freedom, Christian persecution has included discrimination in education and employment and the murder of several pastors. Yet some Iranians are showing a marked interest in Christianity because of believers' response to persecution.

AS YOU PRAY TODAY:

- Ask God to bring expatriate Iranians to Christ so that they can take their faith home to Iran.
- Pray that Iranian believers inside the country will have opportunity to share the Gospel.
- Intercede for creative ways to bring the message of salvation to a darkened land—through radio, literature, and videotapes.

A SOVEREIGN KING

The LORD reigns, let the earth be glad.

PSALM 97:1

There is nothing which we need more than to know the power of the truth "the Lord reigns"; that our God is not a dead God, not an inert God, not an absentee God; but a living God, a Sovereign God, a present God, a working God who is actively engaged in directing, overruling, and shaping the affairs of nations and of men. A new faith in the sovereignty of God will send us back to our tasks with the assurance born of a mighty faith. The Lord reigns, and he will not fail or be discouraged until he has brought forth justice unto victory.

JOHN DANIEL JONES

AS YOU PRAY TODAY:

- Praise God for his control over every aspect of your life.
- Thank him for delivering you from unseen perils and unknown problems.
- Recall and rest in his promises to finish the work he has started in you.

CONFORMED CHARACTER

Those God foreknew he also predestined to be conformed to the likeness of his Son.

ROMANS 8:29

Circumstances do not make character. The noblest character can emerge from the worst surroundings, and moral failures come out of the best. Just where you are, take the things of life as tools, and use them for God's glory; so you will help the kingdom come, and the Master will use the things of life in cutting and polishing you so that there shall some day be seen in you a soul conformed to his likeness.

MALTBIE D. BABCOCK

AS YOU PRAY TODAY:

- Remember that Christ gave his best for you—his life for yours on the cross.
- Give God the best of your life—your highest hopes, your brightest talents.
- Ask him to fill you with his joy and peace and make you more like him.

HONORING THE AGED

"Honor your father and mother"—which is the first commandment with a promise—"that it may go well with you and that you may enjoy long life on the earth."

EPHESIANS 6:2–3

When your parents reach seventy-five or eighty, you may discover that they can no longer care for all of their needs. When grown children must begin to care for their parents, the children may feel isolated and discouraged. Parents may view their caregiver children as constant reminders of what they are no longer capable of doing. Resentment can build. Yet we can be caregivers for our parents and still honor them as God commands. Many resources are available to help both sides cope with the challenges of aging. The best resource for everyone, however, remains prayer.

S.M.H.

AS YOU PRAY TODAY:

- Ask God to give you openness in discussing your parents' future care. Honor them by honoring their decisions.
- Pray for their continued health and mental acuity as well as the courage to ask for help when needed.

"TRIPLE P'S"

Fan into flame the gift of God, which is in you.

2 TIMOTHY 1:6

You see them at worship services every week. We used to call them *Triple P's*—"petrified pew persons." They used to be involved in committees, programs, boards, prayer groups, Bible studies, evangelism, choir, or Sunday School, but now they just warm the same spot in the same pew every week. They lack a vision for their involvement in church, and the flame of their gift is going out. An invitation to a Bible study, a personal request for a volunteer, or even a word of encouragement could fan that flame.

S.M.H.

AS YOU PRAY TODAY:

- Review your commitment and involvement in your church based on your gifts and abilities.
- Ask God to give you a word of encouragement for a "Triple P."
- Pray for older members in your congregation. Ask them about their previous service in the church. You might learn something.

PRAYER WALK

The entire law is summed up in a single command: "Love your neighbor as yourself."

GALATIANS 5:14

Has God placed a prayer burden for your neighborhood on your heart? Wesley L. Duewel says, "Prayer burden begins as an inner impression that you should pray for a known or unknown need. It is a gracious work of the Holy Spirit applying spiritual pressure upon your heart. It is needed and indeed demanded by a situation that cries for God's answer. The burden is the Spirit's personal call for you to intercede."

AS YOU PRAY TODAY:

- Take a walk through your neighborhood and pray for each home as you pass.
- Let the Holy Spirit direct you to specific needs to pray about in each place: salvation, safety, health, a job, etc.
- Enlist others to walk and pray with you and together reclaim your neighborhood for Christ.

THE HORN OF AFRICA

The LORD has anointed me
to preach good news to the poor.
He has sent me to bind up the brokenhearted,
to proclaim freedom for the captives
and release from darkness for the prisoners.
ISAIAH 61:1

Ethnic hostilities have torn the horn of Africa into pieces. An exploitative dictator ruled the nation of Somalia until 1991. Since then there has been no central government in Somalia, and warring factions have brought an end to agriculture and economical growth, choosing instead to trade in narcotics, arms, and food aid. This primarily Muslim republic is anti-Christian. All missionaries were expelled in 1974. The few surviving Somali Christians are severely persecuted for sharing their faith.

AS YOU PRAY TODAY:

- Pray for strength and courage for the Somali believers to stand firm and share the Gospel.
- Most of the country has never heard about Christ. Pray that Christian relief workers will be able to share their witness.
- A few Somali Bibles exist. Pray that these find their way into the hands of believers.

THE POWER OF EL SHADDAI

Is anything too hard for the LORD?

GENESIS 18:14

If God made the heavens, the earth, all people, all creatures, and all things, is there anything too hard for him to do? We should praise him in advance for his mighty works on our behalf. He is already providing for our needs—our food, clothing, and shelter. He's taking care of our financial needs, too, sending showers of unlimited blessing. He has offered us the treasures of his character—his grace to enfold us, his wisdom to guide us, his strength to uphold us. He is El Shaddai—God Almighty. And he loves us very much.

S.M.H.

AS YOU PRAY TODAY:

- Rejoice that nothing is too hard for God.
- Release your worries and cares to his powerful provision.
- Resolve to begin and end each day this week with praise for all that God does and all that he is.

ACKNOWLEDGMENTS

Appleton, George, ed. *The Oxford Book of Prayer.* New York: Oxford University Press, 1988.

Belke, Thomas J. "North Korea's Juche," *The Voice of the Martyrs,* September 2000, p 4. Bartlesville, OK: Voice of the Martyrs, 2000.

Bell, James S., Jr., ed. *They Walked With God.* Chicago: Moody Press, 1993.

Biggs, Dick. *Burn Brightly Without Burning Out.* Gainesville, GA: Biggs Optimal Living Dynamics, 2000.

Cairns, Alan. *Footprints of Faith.* Northern Ireland: Let The Bible Speak, 1989.

Christian Growth Study Bible, New International Version. Grand Rapids, MI: Zondervan Corporation, 1997. Study notes copyright 1997 by Youth With A Mission.

Cleary, Steve. "Carrying the Cross in North Korea," *The Voice of the Martyrs,* September 2000, p 4. Bartlesville, OK: Voice of the Martyrs, 2000.

Copeland, Germaine. *Prayers That Avail Much for Business Professionals.* Tulsa, OK: Harrison House, 1995.

Cowman, Mrs. Charles E. *Streams in the Desert, Volume 2.* Grand Rapids, MI: Zondervan Publishing House, 1977.

Deane, Barbara. *Caring for Your Aging Parents.* Colorado Springs, CO: NavPress, a ministry of the Navigators, 1989.

Dorothy, Dale. "Turn Your Radio On." *World Gospel Mission Call to Prayer,* July/August 2000, pp 28-29. Marion, IN: World Gospel Mission, 2000.

Draper, Edythe, ed. Et.al. *The Almanac of the Christian World.* Wheaton, IL: Tyndale House Publishers, Inc., 1990.

Duewel, Wesley L. *Mighty Prevailing Prayer.* Grand Rapids, MI: Zondervan, 1990. *Touch the World Through Prayer.* Grand Rapids, MI: Zondervan, 1986.

Foster, Richard J. *Prayer: Finding the Heart's True Home.* San Francisco: Harper SanFrancisco, A division of HarperCollinsPublishers, 1992.

Gaither, Bill, P.J. Zondervan, et.al. *Great Gospel Songs and Hymns.* Dallas, TX: Stamps-Baxter Music of the Zondervan Corporation, 1976.

Gaither, Gloria, ed. *What My Parents Did Right.* Nashville, TN: Star Song Publishing Group, 1991.

Hall, Verna M., et.al. *The Christian History of the Constitution of the United States of America.* San Francisco: Foundation for American Christian Education, 1976.

Holmes, Marjorie. "A Psalm for Marriage." *The NIV Women's Devotional Bible 2,* p 1287. Grand Rapids, MI: Zondervan, 1995.

Hosier, Helen, ed. *The Quotable Christian.* Uhrichsville, OH: Barbour Publishing, Inc., 1998.

Huff, Alice, and Eleanor Burr, eds. *A Watered Garden: Devotional Stories From Missionaries.* Grand Rapids, MI: Francis Asbury Press, an imprint of Zondervan Publishing House, 1987.

Hupp, Sarah M., ed. *PUSH! Pray Until Something Happens.* White Plains, NY: Peter Pauper Press, 2000. *Those Who Care Teach.* White Plains, NY: Peter Pauper Press, 1999.

Hybels, Bill, with LaVonne Neff. *Too Busy Not to Pray.* Downers Grove, IL: InterVarsity Press, 1998.

Johnstone, Jill. *You Can Change the World.* Grand Rapids, MI: Zondervan, 1992.
Johnstone, Patrick. *Operation World: The Day-by-Day Guide to Praying for the World.* Grand Rapids, MI: Zondervan, 1993.
Knight, Walter B., ed. *Knight's Treasury of 2,000 Illustrations.* Grand Rapids, MI: Eerdmans Publishing Company, 1963.
Kopp, David and Heather. *Praying the Bible for Your Children.* Colorado Springs, CO: Waterbrook Press, 1997.
Luther, Martin, compiled by Margarete Steiner and Percy Scott. *Day By Day We Magnify Thee.* Philadelphia: Muhlenberg Press, 1946.
Moody, Dwight L. *Still Waters.* London: Marshall Pickering, an Imprint of HarperCollinsPublishers, 1996.
Morgan, G. Campbell. *Great Chapters of the Bible.* Old Tappan, NJ: Evangelical Masterworks, Fleming H. Revell Company, 1935.
Peterson, Eugene H. *Praying With the Psalms.* New York & San Francisco: Harper Collins Publishers and HarperSanFrancisco, 1993.
Peterson, John W., ed. *Great Hymns of the Faith* Grand Rapids, MI: Singspiration Music, of the Zondervan Corporation, 1977.
Prayers From the Heart. Tulsa, OK: Honor Books, 2000.
Rinker, Rosalind. *Prayer: Conversing With God.* Grand Rapids, MI: Zondervan, 1998.
Rodriguez, Jessica. Personal diary of an HCJB working visitor, October 2000. Used by permission.
Sheets, Dutch. *Intercessory Prayer.* Ventura, CA: Regal Books, a Division of Gospel Light, 1996.
Smith, Hamilton, ed. *Gleanings From Thomas Watson.* Morgan, PA: Soli Deo Gloria Publications, 1995.
Spurgeon, Charles H. *Morning and Evening.* Grand Rapids, MI: Zondervan Publishing House, 1980.
Sweeting, George. *Who Said That?* Chicago: Moody Press, 1995.
Swindoll, Charles R., ed. *The Living Insights Study Bible.* Grand Rapids, MI: Zondervan, 1996.
Swofford, Conover. Personal collection. Used by permission.
Tan, Dr. Paul Lee. *Encyclopedia of 7,700 Illustrations: Signs of the Times.* Rockville, MD: Assurance Publishers, 1988.
Washington, James Melvin, PhD., ed. *Conversations With God: Two Centuries of Prayers by African Americans.* New York: HarperPerennial, a Division of HarperCollinsPublishers, 1995.
West, Randy. "The Ministry of Presence." *World Gospel Mission Call to Prayer,* July/August 2000, p 6. Marion, IN: World Gospel Mission, 2000.
White, R.E.O. *You Can Say That Again.* Grand Rapids, MI: Zondervan, 1991.
White, Tom, et.al. "Country Summaries," *The Voice of the Martyrs,* 2001 Special Issue, pp 4-18. Bartlesville, OK: Voice of the Martyrs, 2001.
Wiersbe, Warren W., ed. *Classic Sermons on the Attributes of God.* Kregel Classic Sermon Series. Grand Rapids, MI: Kregel Publications, 1989.
Wilson, Mike. Personal observations of a post-modern teen. Used by permission.
World Almanac and Book of Facts 1999. New York: World Almanac, an Imprint of Pharos Books, A Scripps Howard Company, 1998.